Clinical Cases for Learni
Pediatric Occupational T

A Problem-Based Approach

Diane E. Watson, M.B.A., OTR/L, BCP

Therapy
Skill Builders®

A Harcourt Health Sciences Company

Published by

Therapy
Skill Builders®

A Harcourt Health Sciences Company

ISBN 0761643818

    4 5 6 7 8 9 10 11 12 A B C D E
Printed in the United States of America

To my exceptional parents
and to Gregg, my husband

Contents

Appendixes

Illustrations

Tables

Foreword

In day-to-day clinical practice, pediatric occupational therapists are continually faced with clients who present problems that need to be understood and managed effectively. While most pediatric occupational therapy texts structure learning around theoretical frameworks or medical diagnoses, *Clinical Cases for Learning Pediatric Occupational Therapy: A Problem-Based Approach* is based on the principles of problem-based learning (PBL) and provides a rich source of resource material to enhance learning. To my knowledge, this book is the first of its kind in the field of occupational therapy.

Problem-based learning is recognized by the World Health Organization as a valuable instructional approach in the education of health professionals. Over the last 25 years, since the inception of the first PBL medical school at McMaster University in Canada, problem-based learning has been the subject of much attention, debate, and research. Numerous PBL medical education programs have been implemented worldwide, and many occupational therapy programs in Australia, Canada, Europe, and the United States also have begun to incorporate various elements of problem-based learning into their curricula. Although the PBL approaches do not purport to produce superior health professionals, the subtle benefits of PBL, in terms of cognitive processing and knowledge retention, are well known. In addition, there is no doubt that PBL provides a more active and enjoyable learning environment.

The basic premise of PBL is that a true-to-life clinical problem is used as the stimulus for learning. The author has provided a series of vignettes and case-based problems that cover the spectrum of pediatric practice. The clients in these cases range in age from infancy to middle childhood and present with various medical diagnoses and occupational performance problems in a variety of practice settings. The cases raise important learning issues for further study, such as the use of theoretical frames of reference, models of practice, assessment tools, teamwork collaboration, and state-of-the-art research. Through the exploration of the problem, the learner engages in the process of critical thinking while applying and integrating new information and uses clinical reasoning for determining the role of occupational therapy.

Although *Clinical Cases* primarily was written for occupational therapy educators and their students, practicing pediatric therapists also may find this text a valuable learning resource for professional development and continuing education. In its entirety, this book constitutes an extensive pediatric PBL curriculum that is ideally suited for learning in small groups with a tutor or facilitator; however, individuals and small informal groups of learners can easily design their own program of study using the summary table at the beginning of each module. Learners may use the questions, learning resource lists, and research information provided for each case to guide the learning process and evaluate outcomes.

This book not only serves as a landmark in the history of occupational therapy education, but perhaps more importantly, it provides an exciting opportunity for occupational therapy students and clinicians to gain knowledge and skill in pediatric practice.

Penny Salvatori
Assistant Professor and Chair, BHSc(OT) Programme
McMaster University
Hamilton, Ontario

Acknowledgments

Jordan was an everlasting source of love, laughter, fun, and motivation. His determination and character were evident in everything he did. Physical accomplishments that most children do automatically were things we had to teach Jordan. . . . Jordan gave our entire family, and friends that knew him, a new outlook on life. . . . Unfortunately, not all children with disabilities have the opportunity to grow up and show us what their true potential would have been, but whatever amount of time they are here has a profound influence on those people they touch. Now that we look back at knowing and loving Jordan, we feel he taught us more than we ever have taught him.

—Jordan's family

Jordan's life story is representative of millions of children and their families. This text contains a collection of stories in which children with disabilities teach occupational therapists about pediatric practice. It is my hope that the case method and problem-based approach to learning will enable these young teachers to give you a new outlook on life, as they always have a profound influence on people they touch. Although the stories within this text are hypothetical, they have been created from the collective memories and experiences of a few outstanding therapists.

Rozmin was developed under the ongoing guidance and co-authorship of Barbara Szeliski-Scott, B.Sc.O.T.(c), of the Department of Occupational Therapy, Children's Hospital of Eastern Ontario, Ottawa, Ontario.

Tim (Parts 1 & 2) was written with the assistance and co-authorship of Mary Witoski, B.P.E., B.Sc.O.T.(c). Editorial assistance was provided by Nancy Pollock, M.Sc., OT(C), Assistant Clinical Professor, School of Occupational Therapy and Physiotherapy, McMaster University, Hamilton, Ontario.

Simon was written with the assistance and wisdom of Sylvia Wilson, M.S., B.Sc. OT(c), of the Department of Occupational Therapy at the University of Alberta in Edmonton. Sylvia must be acknowledged for her contributions to the initial drafts of this text and her ongoing mentorship throughout the years.

I am particularly grateful to Gregg Landry, OTR/L, for his editorial assistance during every draft and redraft of this manuscript and for his daily support of "my projects." Pat Rayburn, of The Psychological Corporation, provided editorial leadership, and her literary talents have touched every page of this book. Jack Kasar, Ph.D., of the Department of Occupational Therapy at the University of Scranton in Pennsylvania, provided editorial assistance with *Johan* and *Antonio*. Lyn Silverman, M.Ed., OTR/L, and Joyce Salls, M.S., OTR/L, of the Occupational Therapy Program at Chatham

College in Pittsburgh, Pennsylvania, gave of their time and expertise to review *Antonio* and *Robert*. Heidi Culver, of 2/3 X-PERTS in Scranton, Pennsylvania, working under contract, provided the splint illustrations for the *Gail* and *Rozmin* cases. In 1994, the Canadian Occupational Therapy Foundation awarded this project a publication grant as seed money to assist with the manuscript preparation.

The University of Scranton "aspires to the kind of community for students and faculty in which learning will lead to personal growth and development" and prides itself as a place "where potential becomes achievement" (University of Scranton 1996). Although this project started before my relationship with the university began, the resources and support provided by the University of Scranton, and Dr. Jack Kasar in particular, assured its completion.

Finally, I must acknowledge the educators at the Western Business School at the University of Western Ontario for introducing me to problem-based learning and its potential by role-modeling their version and mastery of the case method.

Introduction

Clinical Cases for Learning Pediatric Occupational Therapy has been designed to meet a variety of needs. The clinical cases prepare occupational therapy students and therapists, intellectually and emotionally, for realistic situations in pediatric practice and empower pediatric clinicians to quickly develop the knowledge and skills required to excel in this specialty. The client stories, issues, and problems provide a realistic context for learning and vivid opportunities for vicarious learning. Although the children, families, and therapists presented are hypothetical, the situations are representative and realistic. Referring to individual cases creates a humanistic context for learning and reinforces the usefulness of newly acquired information, the value of benevolence, and one's ambition to become a pediatric therapist. This experiential learning approach is the unique feature of this book.

Designed for self-directed learning, the problems and challenges presented in this textbook serve as a basis for group discussion. The cases will stimulate interest, dialogue, and debate. The learning issues identified may include understanding scientific issues, applying theoretical models, evaluating functional capacity and potential, designing eclectic intervention, balancing treatment ideals with limited resources, and addressing personal issues that affect clinical practice. The reader quickly acquires knowledge and skills that would otherwise be gained much more slowly.

Module 1

Problem-Based Learning and the Case Method in Occupational Therapy

Tell me, I forget. Show me, I remember.
Involve me, let me do, I understand .

—Author unknown

Problem-based learning (PBL) is an instructional strategy in which the learner works in a self-directed manner toward the understanding or resolution of a practice-related issue. Learning occurs through problem identification, analysis, and resolution. The learning process encourages reflective, critical, and active learning and should speed up the acquisition of clinical reasoning, critical thinking, and judgment. Active learning empowers and inspires learners by providing opportunities for accomplishment. PBL parallels occupational therapy's (a) belief in self-directed behavior; (b) traditional use of purposeful activities to promote learning, insight, skills, and independent performance; and (c) belief that meaningful engagement sanctions diversity and flexibility in adaptation.

Problem-based learning typically requires the use of written vignettes or cases, but they can take the form of videotaped, simulated, or real client interactions (VanLeit 1995). Vignettes include a synopsis of a clinical situation and require the student to do extensive research on the topic of the vignette. Case-based problems contain background information, supply relevant references to streamline analysis, and describe important principles to assist students with problem identification and resolution analysis. Case-based problems are different from case studies and histories in that they engage the learner by presenting issues that require attention and action. The authors of the cases do not provide the answers but simply guide the reader through part of the process. VanLeit affirms that the case or problem format requires students to select resources, condense information from multiple disciplines, develop and use clinical reasoning skills; therefore, students feel more comfortable with uncertain or ambiguous clinical situations, and they discover important civic issues that are pertinent (VanLeit 1994, 3).

Although the problems portrayed are hypothetical, the issues are representational, and their realism provides a context for novice therapists to practice all of the cognitive steps and professional behaviors required of a successful practitioner. The problems are structured to stimulate curiosity and inquiry, and to provide ample opportunity for individuals to determine the focus and intensity of their learning experience. Because the style and scope of practice vary over time among facilities and among therapists, these cases are not meant to be a single example of effective practice or the only guidelines for clinical competency.

Because occupational therapy is as much an art as it is a science, and because each client is unique and multidimensional, occupational therapy graduates require a cognitive model for clinical reasoning and professional skills (Côtè 1993). In an industry and profession characterized by rapid change and growth, future practitioners will need professional skills and educational preparation that include the process and content of learning. The information taught today will not be the knowledge of tomorrow, so teachers must ignite a passion in students for lifelong learning (Vargo 1994). *Clinical Cases for Learning Pediatric Occupational Therapy* attempts to ensure that students and therapists possess the knowledge, skills, and passion for learning that will result in greater success in fieldwork, in professional practice, and throughout their careers in pediatrics.

Professionals in pediatric service undoubtedly experience consternation when confronted with the wealth of information characteristic of an established specialty. Therapists may simultaneously feel eager to learn, unsure of their skills, and discouraged by the amount of time and energy required to gain experience. *Clinical Cases* provides information and role models for quick and efficient skill development, addressing the needs of entry-level therapists, clinicians re-entering the profession, and practitioners entering pediatrics. "Case studies of unusually visionary yet well-grounded exemplars of good practice may present the ideal middle ground between the unfettered fantasies of the dreamers and the unimaginative practices of the uninspired" (Shulman 1992, 8).

The cases presented in this text are designed to meet a variety of needs. Experienced pediatric clinicians who are interested in enhancing their service delivery will find *Clinical Cases for Learning Pediatric Occupational Therapy* useful for self-evaluation and professional development. The cases may be used as a vehicle for staff and team development by stimulating inquiry, dialogue, and sharing. Sole-charge therapists who lack more experienced colleagues to guide their learning and skill development can use this text as a self-study manual. Instructors and employers may select and assign cases from this text and ask applicants and students to develop and demonstrate their knowledge, skills, and abilities.

Learning in PBL occurs through independent investigation and can be supplemented by group sessions or tutorials. The process of problem resolution encourages reflective, critical, and active learning and reinforces the integration and applicability of new information. Advocates and researchers suggest that through PBL the learner

- acquires a relevant and integrated body of knowledge,
- bridges the gap between theory and practice more easily,
- develops superior interpersonal skills,
- gains proficiency in information management,
- acquires a holistic frame of reference,
- forms life-long learning skills, and
- is more satisfied and interested in the subject matter

(Albanese and Mitchell 1993; Boud and Feletti 1991; Sadlo et al. 1994; Walton and Matthews 1989).

The Role of the Student

Developing the professional skills and work habits of an autonomous professional is a demanding responsibility. Individuals who are accustomed to didactic, lecture-style education may initially suffer the shock of transition. If the transition is not made during the academic phase of preparation, it will most likely occur during fieldwork or upon graduation. This is a natural transition process.

Traditional pediatric textbooks are organized according to established theoretical frameworks or medical taxonomies. The processes of information integration and appropriate clinical application are left to the reader. While these texts typically identify the need for clinical reasoning, their organization does not provide a context for the reader to develop the necessary reasoning skills. Traditional textbooks and lecture-based instruction are adequate for the acquisition of information, but skills and abilities must be developed, practiced, and refined in a context that closely approximates reality. Students and therapists must learn to appropriately apply theory in complex situations and to balance the realities of clinical practice and the ideals portrayed in textbooks. Occupational therapy theory and practice can and should be experienced simultaneously (Cracknell 1992).

The client cases contained in this text require the student to access, collect, and evaluate information from sources that a pediatric therapist must use. These sources include colleagues, library media, community resources, standardized test manuals, and product suppliers. The satisfaction derived from becoming familiar with a new client, solving unique problems, planning intervention, and modeling professional skills cannot be overestimated.

Research findings of student therapists, satisfaction with problem-based learning (PBL) is overwhelmingly positive. Approximately 70%–83% of medical students who initially did not elect to participate in PBL changed their minds after experiencing PBL (Moore 1991). Five different research studies evaluating satisfaction ratings indicate that 70%–88% of students were satisfied after taking a PBL module or course (Davis et al. 1992; Eisenstaedt et al. 1990; Moore-West et al. 1989; West and West 1987).

PBL requires students to solve the problem presented in each case and to assume responsibility for the scope, depth, and direction of their educational experience. Many students initially have difficulty with this concept and feel that they do not have enough information or experience to make decisions. One of the valuable lessons learned from this process is that professionals must make informed decisions with limited knowledge. It is important "to see ignorance as a challenge to further learning rather than as a cause for shame," and to "recognize that nothing is ever learned to finality"(Walton and Matthews 1989).

To assist students with planning an educational experience, each module of this text begins with a summary table that describes the content of the cases. Information regarding the client age, primary diagnosis, area of practice, frame of reference, clinical issues, tests used, and location and scope of practice are included. This table will enable you to design your program of study and anticipate case issues and challenges. Each vignette or case is followed by study questions, vocabulary words, resources, and research.

As the student becomes more accustomed to PBL, self-assessment becomes automatic and motivating. Classroom discussions, group work in tutorials, and study groups will require that participants nurture and teach others, manage conflict, and give and receive formative feedback. The case approach to learning is a strong, effective technique due to analysis and to group discussion, in particular (Rakich, Longest, and Darr et al. 1987, xvi).

For more productive learning in the group discussions, consider the following:

> Although independent investigation is important to professional development, do not hesitate to share information and discuss the case with others. Cooperation will enhance the learning experience and result in improved teaching ability. Autonomy and mutual respect may be developed simultaneously. Informal study groups or formal tutorials aid in this process. Lawlor and Henderson (1989) indicate that approximately 70% of pediatric occupational therapists work as part of a team.

> Everyone has different skills and learning styles. Make a conscious effort to contribute to the development and learning of others. There is a difference between quality and quantity in group participation; plan the content and timing of your contributions, and consider the impact of your comments on others.

No group participant should be a silent observer. Serious and extensive preparation by everyone present will improve the value, scope, and intensity of group discussion (Rakich et al. 1987). The learning outcome is positively correlated with the amount of effort devoted to case analysis.

Colleagues will have the opportunity to support, question, or dispute your ideas. This is the value of teams. Expect and tolerate challenges to your views and be willing to offer ideas and recommendations to colleagues. Practicing clinicians are required to clearly articulate their approach and rationale and to accept criticism.

When recommendations do not seem reasonable, it is each member's responsibility to provide feedback. Individual insights may require that members of the group reevaluate their conclusions and recommendations. However, insights from others in the group may require that individual students reevaluate their own conclusions and recommendations. This interaction is the value of teams that learn together.

Group dynamics and the development of skilled participants are the responsibility of all group members. It is everyone's responsibility to be a facilitator, moderator, role model, and mentor.

Occupational therapy students who have used the cases in this text were asked about their impressions about PBL and the case method and whether they prefer traditional lecture-style learning or the self-directed and group learning format. They made the following comments:

> I feel that this style of learning is much more enjoyable because the students are active participants. I also feel that because the student has to play such an active role in the learning process, much more of the knowledge is retained. Its almost as if PBL is hands-on learning—or as close to it as you can get . . . . At first, I thought that I preferred the traditional lecture. Now after eight weeks of PBL, I definitely prefer the self-directed and group-learning format. I feel that PBL prepares me for the challenges of clinical internships because I have been able to retain so much more of the information that I have learned. I have much more confidence in my knowledge and lots of resources as well as research skills* (Mazzulo 1995).

> In traditional [lecture-style learning] you learn for the test[;] in PBL you learn for yourself* (Hagy 1995).

> PBL prepares the student for clinical experience by teaching the student[s] ways to answer their own questions* (Erskine 1995).

---

*Excerpts taken from students' evaluations of *Pediatric Occupational Therapy: A Problem-Based Approach to Learning*. Reprinted with permission. Mazzulo, G. M., E. A. Hagy, E. M. Erskine, M. J. Hance, and I Salcedo. 1995. Nova Southeastern University, Ft. Lauderdale, FL. Printed with permission.

The student really blossoms throughout the course as he/she expands on his/her self-directed learning* (Hance 1995).

PBL is the wave of the future for OT programs! When the time came for hands-on experiences, I felt more confident and knowledgeable and was able to approach a child with no fear* (Salcedo 1995).

The Role of the Instructor

The fundamental challenge of instructors in professional programs is to ensure that students develop the knowledge, skills, and abilities required for success in their chosen field. Occupational therapy instructors have developed strategies to teach the content base required for practice but continue to seek methods to develop professionalism and nurture skills in clinical reasoning, problem solving, lifelong learning, and holistic care. Royeen (1995), Sadlo and colleagues (1994), and VanLeit (1995) argue that PBL will prepare reflective critical thinkers with the clinical reasoning skills required for future practice.

PBL strategy differs from traditional beliefs about education in many important ways. It is these differences that dictate the new roles and responsibilities of instructors and students. The following table lists the differences.

Table 1.1 Comparison of Two Learning Strategies

Problem-Based Learning	Traditional
Contextual learning	Rote memorization
Multimedia resources	Centrality of the textbook
Learn through inquiry and research	Lecture and listen
Active learners	Passive learners
Student-directed	Teacher-directed
Student has ultimate responsibility	Teacher as ultimate authority
Focus on process	Focus on content
Trust learners	Structure learning
Continuous learning	Episodic learning

---

*Excerpts taken from students' evaluations of *Pediatric Occupational Therapy: A Problem-Based Approach to Learning*. Reprinted with permission. Mazzulo, G. M., E. A. Hagy, E. M. Erskine, M. J. Hance, and I Salcedo. 1995. Nova Southeastern University, Ft. Lauderdale, FL.

Students' abilities to assume responsibility for their own education depend on prior experiences and opportunities. In this text, the cases include questions, new vocabulary, suggested resources, and theoretical information to guide individuals in directing their educational experiences. Facilitating access to resources and information is critical in the early stages of a PBL pediatrics course. Each student should become familiar with the pediatric section of the library, CD-ROM database searches, and should acquire a personal library of reference material and supplier catalogs. Each student must analyze problems assigned, either individually or as part of a group, and come to class prepared to exchange ideas, perceptions, and experiences.

The PBL classroom environment is significantly different from the traditional teacher-directed lecture format. PBL instructors must believe in students' abilities to assume responsibility; create opportunities for group dialogue; nurture self-directed learning, professional behaviors, and interpersonal skills; and create a classroom environment that is supportive of these objectives. The classroom must be a forum for the presentation and defense of opinions, critical analysis of alternatives, and the development of a holistic and eclectic approach to therapy. Rather than lecturing or providing solutions, the instructor guides, probes, and supports the students' initiatives and stimulates group dialogue. This instructional format is based on the concept that "there exists too much for any one person to learn and that tasks need to be shared between students" (Walton and Matthews 1989, 544).

The instructor must develop the physical and psychological climate of the program or course and create safe opportunities for cooperative and interactive learning (Knowles 1985). The PBL classroom requires openness to promote disclosure and critical analysis and to ensure collaboration, inquiry, creativity, and competence. The first few classes or group discussions are critical for defining the boundaries of acceptable behavior and establishing a learning environment (Kisfalvi 1993). Group members need to subdue monopolistic conversationalists while nurturing apprehensive introverts. To develop a healthy internal group climate, teams of students require time to experiment with dynamics and structure. By *learning* as a team, skills and abilities may translate to *working* as a team (Royeen 1994).

Occupational therapy PBL educators use a number of cooperative group formats and structures, including the following (Watson and West 1996):

- Groups of five to nine students with assigned or self-selected members and faculty or community therapist facilitators
- Student study groups without expert facilitators
- Large group discussions (of more than 30 students), student forums, and symposiums
- Interdisciplinary seminars, tutorials, and labs

Educators using PBL rate their curriculums higher in teaching clinical reasoning, humanistic qualities, and preventive care than do educators using a conventional curriculum (Post and Drop 1990). A number of studies document faculty satisfaction, particularly the perceived benefits of greater student contact (Albanese and Mitchell 1993).

"If we observe the process which we call instruction, we see two parties conjointly engaged the learner and the teacher. The object of both is the same, but their relations to the work to be done are different . . . [I]t follows that he [the learner] is in fact his own teacher, and . . . that learning is self-teaching . . . . The teachers part then in the process of instruction is that of a guide, director, or superintendent of the operations by which the pupil teaches himself" (Payne 1883).

References

Albanese, M. A., and S. Mitchell. 1993. Problem-based learning: A review of literature in its outcomes and implementation issues. *Academic Medicine* 68:52–81.

Boud, D., and G. Feletti. 1991. *The challenge of problem-based learning.* London: Kogan Page.

Côtè, M. 1993. Case method, case teaching and the making of a manager. In *Case method research and application: Innovation through cooperation*, edited by H. E. Klein. Needham, MA: World Association for Case Method Research and Application.

Cracknell, E. 1992. Learning through doing. *British Journal of Occupational Therapy* 55:411.

Davis, W. K., R. Nairn, M. E. Pain, R. M. Anderson, and M. S. Oh. 1992. Effects of expert and non-expert facilitators on the small-group process and on student performance. *Academic Medicine* 67:407–74.

Eisenstaedt, R. S., W. E. Barry, and K. Glanz. 1990. Problem-based learning: Cognitive retention and cohort traits of randomly selected participants and decliners. *Academic Medicine* 65 (Supplement):11–12.

Kisfalvi, V. 1993. The creation of a "safe place" in the classroom: An essential requirement for case method teaching. In *Innovation through cooperation*, edited by H. E. Klein. Needham, MA: World Association for Case Method Research and Application.

Knowles, M. S. 1985. *Andragogy in action.* San Francisco: Jossey-Bass.

Lawlor, M. C., and A. Henderson. 1989. A descriptive study of the clinical practice patterns of occupational therapists working with infants and young children. *American Journal of Occupational Therapy* 43:755–64.

Moore, G. T. 1991. The effect of compulsory participation of medical students in problem-based learning. *Medical Education* 25:140–43.

Moore-West, M., D. L. Harrington, S. P. Mennin, A. Kaufman, and B. J. Skipper. 1989. Distress and attitudes toward the learning environment: Effects of a curriculum innovation. *Teaching and Learning in Medicine* 1:151–57.

Payne, J. 1883. *Lectures in the science and art of education.* Boston: Willard Small.

Post, G. J., and M. J. Drop. 1990. Perceptions of the content of the medical curriculum at the medical faculty in Maastricht: A comparison with traditional curricula in the Netherlands. In *Innovation in medical education: An evaluation of its present status,* edited by Z. Nooman, H. G. Schmidt, and E. S. Ezza, 64–75. New York: Springer.

Rakich, J. S., B. B. Longest, and K. Darr. 1987. *Cases in health services management. 2d ed.* Owing Mills, MD: AUPHA Press Rynd Communications.

Royeen, C. 1994. Problem-based learning in action: Key points for practical use. *Education: Special Interest Section Newsletter of the American Occupational Therapy Association* 4:1–2.

Royeen, C. 1995. A problem-based learning curriculum for occupational therapy education. *American Journal of Occupational Therapy* 49:338–46.

Sadlo, G., D. W. Piper, and P. Agnew. 1994. Problem-based learning in the development of an occupational therapy curriculum, Part 1: The process of problem-based learning. *British Journal of Occupational Therapy* 27:49–54.

Shulman, L. S. 1992. Toward a pedagogy of cases. In *Case methods in teacher education,* ed. by J. H. Shulman. New York: Teachers College.

University of Scranton, 1996. *University of Scranton Undergraduate Catalogue.* Scranton, PA: University Press.

VanLeit, B. 1994. Problem-based learning: A strategy for teaching undergraduate occupational therapy students. *Education: Special Interest Section Newsletter of the American Occupational Therapy Association* 4:3–4.

VanLeit, B. 1995. Using the case method to develop clinical reasoning skills in problem-based learning. *American Journal of Occupational Therapy* 49:349–53.

Vargo, J. 1994. Igniting a passion for learning: The University of Alberta's Jim Vargo is the 1994 Canadian professor of the year. *New Trails* 49:8–9.

Walton, H. J., and M. B. Matthews. 1989. Essentials of problem-based learning. *Medical Education* 23:542–58.

Watson, D., and D. West. 1996. Using problem-based learning to improve educational outcomes. *Occupational Therapy International* 3:1–17.

West, D. A., and M. M. West. 1987. Problem-based learning of psychopathology in a traditional curriculum using multiple conceptual models. *Medical Education* 21:151–56.

Module 2

*There is no cement like interest, no stimulus
like a hint of practical consideration.*

—Flexner 1910

Anwar and Annette	Bernadette
Developmental Stage Theorists	Pediatric Frames of Reference
Occupational Therapy	Problem-Based teaching
Developmental Theorists	and learning
Pediatric Occupational Performance	Board Certification in Pediatrics

Child Development and Theoretical Concepts Clinical Cases

Anwar and Annette

As set forth by Anne Cronin Mosey, PhD, OTR, FAOTA (1970), frames of reference provide methodological organization of theoretical and practical material in sequences needed for problem identification and solution in practice. *

—Jim Hinojosa, Paula Kramer

Anwar and Annette are beginning their fieldwork internship at the Rehabilitation Center for Children. On the first day of orientation, their clinical supervisor gives them a joint work assignment. Anwar and Annette are expected (1) to prepare a 15-minute presentation on two different developmental theories, and (2) to compile a list of children's developmental abilities from infancy to adolescence. They are to make their presentation to the staff occupational therapists at their regular meeting the following week and use the completed list during the remainder of their internship.

The clinical supervisor identifies three learning objectives for this exercise. Anwar and Annette must work together to become familiar with

- the staff of the occupational therapy department,
- resources and materials in the department, and
- developmental expectations of children.

Anwar and Annette have never met but share a lot in common. They both have one year of academic training remaining and very limited exposure to children in their personal lives. They meet for a few minutes on Monday and agree on a research strategy. They decide that on Monday night and Tuesday they will work independently to compile information from various personal and departmental resources. They will meet again Tuesday night to share their information, select the presentation topic, and determine which resources have not yet been tapped. From Wednesday to Friday, both students will continue their research and meet on Saturday to prepare their presentation.

---

*Reprinted by permission of the publisher. From *Frames of Reference for Pediatric Occupational Therapy*, p. 3. Hinojosa, J., P. Kramer. Copyright © 1993 by Williams & Wilkins.

Anwar has two nephews and offers to talk to his sister regarding the children's developmental milestones. Annette is determined to contribute information that is equally as interesting as her partner's, but she will have to rely on information from literature. Their clinical supervisor suggests that the students review textbooks on human development, watch videos on normal movement, and examine standardized test manuals for normative data. Both students are given unlimited access to the department's resources and the center's library.

On Monday night, Annette reviews her textbook on child development. She is familiar with many theorists and considers which two theories she wants to investigate further. As Annette reads, she outlines possible presentation topics. The following chart contains several theorists that she considered, along with their theories.

Table 2.1 Theorists

Developmental Stage Theorists	Freud: psychosexual development
	Erikson: ego adaptation
	Piaget: cognitive development
	Kohlberg: moral development
Occupational Therapy Developmental Theorists	Gilfoyle, Grady, and Moore: spatiotemporal adaptation
	Reilly: play as exploratory learning
	Llorens: facilitating growth and development
	Mosey: occupational behavior

Next, Annette draws seven tables to assist with compiling information on developmental competencies and begins to fill in some of the blanks.

The Challenge

Assume that Anwar and Annette's challenges and responsibilities are your own. Work independently, with a partner, or in a small group to complete the first assignment, a 15-minute presentation. Be prepared to present the findings in class to the occupational therapy department. In preparation for a meeting with a partner or small group, conduct independent research for the second assignment and make a list of children's developmental milestones. Use the following tables that Annette constructed to help compile information.

Table 2.2 Neonate—0 to 1 Month

Self-Care	Play
Opens mouth to stimulus.	*Physiological flexion.*

Table 2.3 Infant–1 to 12 Months

Physical Development	*Rolls prone to supine.*
Cognitive Development	
Language and Speech Development	
Psychosocial Development	
Self-Help	*Swallows strained or pureed foods.*

Table 2.4 Toddler–1 to 3 Years

Physical Development	
Cognitive Development	
Language and Speech Development	
Psychosocial Development	
Self-Help	*Toilet training.* *Helps with simple household chores.*

Table 2.5 Preschooler–3 to 5 Years

Physical Development	*Balances on one foot for 5 seconds (~3¹/₂ years).*
Cognitive Development	
Language and Speech Development	
Psychosocial Development	
Self-Help	*Opens food containers (~ 4-5 years).*

Table 2.6 Middle Childhood–6 to 8 Years

Self-Care	Productive Activities	Leisure Play
Ties shoelaces (~6 years).	*Begins school.*	

Table 2.7 Early Adolescence–9 to 11 Years

Self-Care	Productive Activities	Leisure Play
Strong peer bonding.	*Writes essays.*	*Peer group socials.*

Table 2.8 Adolescence–12 Years and Up

Self-Care	Productive Activities	Leisure Play
First bank account.		

Reference

Flexner, A. 1910. *Medical education in the United States and Canada: A report for the Carnegie Foundation for the advancement of teaching.* Bulletin No. 4.

Learning Resources

Literature

Alexander, R., Boehme, R., and B. Cupps. 1993. *Normal development of functional motor skills: The first year of life.* Tucson, AZ: Therapy Skill Builders.

Case-Smith, J., A. S. Allen, and P. Pratt. 1996. *Occupational therapy for children.* 3d ed. St. Louis: Mosby.

Craig, G. J. 1986. *Human development.* 4th ed. Englewood Cliffs, NJ: Prentice-Hall.

Erhardt, R. P. 1994. *Developmental hand dysfunction: Theory, assessment and treatment,* 2d ed. Tucson, AZ: Therapy Skill Builders.

Gilfoyle, E. M., A. P. Grady, and J. C. Moore. 1990. *Children adapt: A theory of sensorimotor-sensory development.* 2d ed. Thorofare, NJ: Slack.

Lewis, M., and F. Volkmar. 1990. *Clinical aspects of child and adolescent development: An introductory synthesis of developmental concepts and clinical experience.* 3d ed. Philadelphia: Lea & Febiger.

Llorens, L. A. 1970. 1969 Eleanor Clark Slagle Lecture: Facilitating growth and development, the promise of occupational therapy. *American Journal of Occupational Therapy* 24:93.

Morris, S. E., and M. D. Klein. 1987. *Pre-feeding skills: A comprehensive resource for feeding development.* Tucson, AZ: Therapy Skill Builders.

Mosey, A. C. 1986. *Psychosocial components of occupational therapy.* New York: Raven Press.

Reilly, M. 1974. *Play as exploratory learning: Studies of curiosity behavior.* Beverly Hills, CA: Sage Publications.

Short-DeGraff, M. A. 1988. *Human development for occupational and physical therapists.* Baltimore: Williams & Wilkins.

Videos

Goudy, K., and J. Fetzer. 1988. *Infant motor development: A look at the phases.* Tucson, AZ: Therapy Skill Builders.

Telepool. *The first 365 days in the life of a child.* Princeton, NJ: Films for the Humanities and Sciences.

Standardized Tests (See Appendix A for more detail.)

Alberta Infant Motor Scale

Developmental Test of Visual-Motor Integration, 3rd Revision

Hawaii Early Learning Profile-Revised

Miller Assessment of Preschoolers

Peabody Developmental Motor Scales

Pediatric Evaluation of Disability Inventory

Vineland Adaptive Behavior Scales

Bernadette

Bernadette has just received notice that she passed the American Occupational Therapy Association (AOTA) board examination for certification in pediatrics. By 1995, 284 occupational therapists earned this designation (Joe 1995). AOTA has offered certification as a pediatric specialist since 1990, following a Representative Assembly resolution in 1989 (Joe 1990). The objectives of this certification program include

- supporting quality care by promoting the development of specialized knowledge, best practice, education, and research in pediatrics;
- assisting consumers in identifying therapists with expertise; and
- providing assistance and support for pediatric occupational therapy career development

(AOTA 1994).

Bernadette reflects on her accomplishments. Yesterday she was asked to discuss pediatric frames of reference and models of practice with the occupational therapy students at ABC University. The Rehabilitation Center for Children (RCC), Bernadette's employer, has a close relationship with the local university, and RCC provides educational support to their students. The department of occupational therapy professors at ABC University use a problem-based approach to learning, to empower students to self-direct the development of their knowledge, skills, and abilities. Bernadette is familiar with the use of problem-based learning and incorporates this educational strategy within the clinical environment.

Bernadette prepares for her visit to the university by defining student learning objectives. Upon completion of the session, the students would be able to

- describe the holistic, client-centered approach used by occupational therapists in the multidisciplinary teams at RCC; and
- practice correctly applying occupational therapy frames of reference and models of practice to specific pediatric clients.

Bernadette designs eight short case-based problems to provide a context for learning these pediatric frames of reference.

Table 2.9 Eight Case-Based Problems

	Theoretical Concepts and Premises	Objectives of Evaluation and Intervention	Case-Based Problem	Resolving the Problem
1. Behavioral Approach			Sal, 5 years old, attends a preschool program for autistic students. His teacher would like some behavior management strategies.	
2. Bio-mechanical			Marianne was admitted during an acute episode of juvenile rheumatoid arthritis (JRA).	
3. Cognitive Perceptual			Barry sustained a mild traumatic brain injury at 7 years of age. Despite good motor control, he has great difficulty with reading, printing, and drawing.	
4. Coping			Donna, 13 years old, attempted suicide. Her only parent is alcoholic.	
5. Group Work Model			Debbie is a 15-year-old girl who seeks solitude. She is a ritualistic exerciser with anorexia nervosa.	

	Theoretical Concepts and Premises	Objectives of Evaluation and Intervention	Case-Based Problem	Resolving the Problem
6. Model of Human Occupation			Peter was diagnosed with a C8 spinal cord injury following a motor vehicle accident 1 month ago. He is 7 years old and wants to be discharged as soon as possible.	
7. Motor Control Model			Aaron, 6 years old, is having difficulty learning to print. He was diagnosed with spastic diplegia at 1 year.	
8. Sensory Integration			Zita is an 8-year-old student in third grade who is unable to hop, skip, somersault, or ride a bicycle.	

The Challenge

You are an occupational therapy (OT) student at ABC University. For each model of practice, describe the conceptual framework, therapeutic objectives of evaluation and treatment, and how you, as an OT, would apply these principles to address the problems presented in the cases.

New Terminology

anorexia nervosa

autism

C8 spinal cord injury

juvenile rheumatoid arthritis (JRA)

multidisciplinary team

spastic diplegia

Learning Resources

Ayres, A. J. 1985. *Sensory integration and the child.* Los Angeles: Western Psychological.

Bly, L. 1991. A historical and current view of the basis of NDT. *Pediatric Physical Therapy* 3:131–53.

Boehm, R. 1990. *Approach to treatment of the baby.* Tucson, AZ: Therapy Skill Builders.

Canadian Association of Occupational Therapists. 1991. *Position paper on the role of occupational therapy in pediatrics.* Toronto: CAOT.

Case-Smith, J. 1994. Defining the specialization of pediatric occupational therapy. *American Journal of Occupational Therapy* 48:791–802.

Case-Smith J., A. S. Allen, and P. Pratt. 1996. *Occupational therapy for children.* 3d ed. St. Louis: Mosby.

Fisher, A. C., E. A. Murray, and A. C. Bundy. 1991. *Sensory integration: Theory and practice.* Philadelphia: F. A. Davis.

Kaplan, H. I., B. J. Sadock, and J. A. Grebb. 1994. *Synopsis of psychiatry.* 7th ed. Baltimore: Williams & Wilkins.

Kielhofner, G. 1992. *Conceptual foundation of occupational therapy.* Philadelphia: F. A. Davis.

Kramer, J., and J. Hinojosa. 1993. *Frames of reference for pediatric occupational therapy.* Baltimore: Williams & Wilkins.

Snider, L. M. 1991. *Sensory integration therapy.* Tucson, AZ: Therapy Skill Builders.

Short-DeGraff, M. A. 1988. *Human development for occupational and physical therapists.* Baltimore: Williams & Wilkins.

Zeitlin, S., G. G. Williamson, and W. P. Rosenblatt. 1987. The coping with stress model: A counseling approach for families with a handicapped child. *Journal of Counseling and Development* 65:443–46.

References

American Occupational Therapy Association. 1994. *Pediatric specialty certification program.* Bethesda, MD: AOTA.

Joe, B. 1990. AOTA initiates a specialty certification in pediatrics. *OT Week* (4 November): 24.

Joe, B. 1995. Specialty certification confers unique benefits. *OT Week* (24 September): 26–27.

Module 3

Infancy Clinical Cases

	Johan	Kari	Antonio
PBL Approach	Case method	Vignette	Case method
Age	7 months	7 months	16 months
Primary Diagnosis	Premature	Substance-exposed	Cerebral palsy
Area of Practice	Screening	Screening	Initial evaluation
Location of Practice	Home	Home	Home
Frame of Reference	Developmental Motor control Sensory integration	Developmental Human occupation	Biomechanical Motor control
Performance Area	Activities of daily living (ADL) and Play	Activities of daily living (ADL) and Play	Activities of daily living (ADL) and Play
Performance Components	Motor Cognitive Social-emotional Self-help	Motor Cognitive Social-emotional Self-help	Motor Cognitive Social-emotional Self-help
Performance Context	Young single parent Low-income First-and-only child	Single parent Low-income Drug culture	Spanish speaking Large extended family One sibling
Clinical Issues	Multidisciplinary team	Transdisciplinary team Values and Attitudes	Interdisciplinary team Family-focused services
Occupational Therapy Tests	AIMS HELP-R PDMS	To be determined	COPM, Denver II, HELP-R, PDMS

Alberta Infant Motor Scale (AIMS); Canadian Occupational Performance Measure (COPM); Hawaii Early Learning Profile-Revised (HELP-R); Peabody Developmental Motor Scales (PDMS).

Infancy Clinical Cases

Johan

*Although we want to know about the needs of the child, those
needs are important only within the context of the concerns, priorities,
and resources of the family. We recognize parents as active and equal
partners in making decisions and as participants in every step of the process. **

—Miller and Roid, 1994

Background

Johan was born at 34 weeks gestation. His 1-minute Apgar score was 5, and his 5-minute score was 7. Although his birth weight was 1750 grams, his 3-month weight was in the 50 percentile for his corrected age. Dr. Lu at the Well Baby Center recommended a developmental assessment for 7-month-old Johan.

For the first month after discharge from the maternity ward, Johan and his mother lived with his maternal grandmother. Johan had to be fed and bathed, and his mother was petrified to do either of these activities alone. Johan cried so much it was hard to tell if he was hungry, tired, or sad. By the end of the third month, Johan's mother began searching for an apartment. Although they didn't have much money or furniture, Johan and his mother moved into social-assistance housing.

Therapists visit Johan

While waiting for the early intervention workers, Johan's mother nervously waits and wonders what early intervention might mean. When the two therapists arrive, the mother answers the door, and the visitors introduce themselves. Barbara, one of the therapists, has been a pediatric occupational therapist for almost a year. Her partner and colleague, Maria, has been an early intervention physical therapist for 5 years. Now they work as a team with the ABC Infant and Toddler Program (ABC-ITP) to assess children's motor, cognitive, communication, social-emotional, and self-help skills and to provide home-based, family-focused services. ABC-ITP offers comprehensive,

---

*Miller, L. J., and G. H. Roid. 1994. *The T.I.M.E. Toddler and Infant Motor Evaluation: A Standardized Assessment*. Tucson, AZ: Therapy Skill Builders. Reprinted with permission.

27

multidisciplinary early intervention services to enhance the development of infants and toddlers with disabilities. To qualify for services, infants must be medically insured, qualify for Medicaid, or meet the eligibility criteria for Part H of the Individuals with Disabilities Education Act (IDEA), Public Law (P.L.) 101–476 1990.

Barbara: Dr. Lu's referral to ABC-ITP indicates that Johan was premature and of low birth weight when he was born. Is this correct?

Mother: Yes. Why is that important?

Barbara: Dr. Lu and the staff at ABC-ITP just want to ensure that Johan is healthy. His birth status places him at risk for developmental delays, so it's important to make sure he is all right. How do you think Johan is doing?

Mother: He seems to be fine to me. He doesn't cry as much as he did when he was born. He watches me all the time, smiles a lot, and likes to babble. Don't you think that means he's healthy?

As the parent interview progresses, the therapists determine that Mother was employed part-time as a cashier until her second trimester. Although she dropped out of high school one year ago, Mother indicates that she is interested in returning to school. Mother says that her friends visit regularly and enjoy playing with Johan. She indicates that she learns most things about children by reading and is not concerned about Johan's development. The therapists ask Mother to identify her own strengths and needs, in relation to promoting Johan's development, and to rank order them according to their importance (1 = most important, 5 = least important). Her responses are shown in the chart that follows.

Table 3.1 Parent's Strengths and Needs

Strengths	Rank	Needs	Rank
"I spend a lot of time with Johan."	3	"I need more experience."	2
"I love my son."	1	"I don't have very much money for toys and things."	1
"I read about what to do."	5		
"I play with him all the time."	4		
"I take Johan to the clinic."	2		

Meanwhile, Johan is lying semireclined on a pillow, actively and intently sucking from his bottle and inspecting the two new faces.

Barbara: Does Johan eat any solid foods?

Mother: Yes, he likes baby food and bananas. I haven't given him crackers or cookies yet. Should I be doing that now?

Barbara: Do you have any cereal and crackers? We can try them to see how well he does. Why don't you start with some baby food to show me how well Johan eats?

Mother places Johan in an old high chair and begins by feeding her child some packaged pudding with a spoon. Johan cleans the spoon off with his upper lip and occasionally grabs for the utensil. After three or four spoonfuls, he begins drooling some food out of the lateral borders (corners) of his lips.

Johan grabs for the small piece of cereal as soon as it is placed in front of him but is unable to retrieve it. Eventually, Johan catches the piece of cereal in the palm of his fist. Although he brings it to his lips, he is unable to place the small piece of food into his mouth. Mother helps, and Johan eventually munches the cereal piece with up-and-down jaw and tongue movements. Barbara takes a small piece of cracker, lightly soaks it with liquid, and hands it to Mother. Mother gives it to her son, and Johan eats the piece without difficulty. As they progress, it is determined that Johan can safely munch on small pieces of cracker. Barbara places a small plastic cup in front of Johan. He uses both hands to pick it up, bangs it on the table twice, and laughs. Next, he brings the rim of the cup to his open mouth and protruding tongue. When snack time is over, Maria pulls out a bag of infant toys and asks if she can have some of Johan's toys. Mother returns with a rubber noisemaker toy and rattle.

Maria: We would like to observe Johan playing. It is during play that children most often display their skills and knowledge. Could you place Johan on his back on the floor in front of you?

It is Maria's personal preference to begin the evaluation by placing a child in supine. This position enables the infant to observe the therapist while maintaining eye contact with the mother. Many infants with disabilities have great difficulty while in the prone position or while sitting, and Maria did not want to upset Johan or mother. Although the supine position may be challenging, it is not as threatening.

Mother reaches out her hands to Johan as he sits in the high chair, and he immediately raises his arms in anticipation of being picked up. Mother lays him on the floor and presents him with his rattle. He lies with his head and trunk aligned, hands in midline and chin tucked, while he watches and plays with this toy. As he becomes more excited, Johan kicks his feet. Maria asks Mother to hold the rattle at Johan's knees and then at his feet to see if he can reach that far. Johan uses his abdominal muscles, hip abduction, and hip external rotation to grab the rattle. When Mother tickles his toes, Johan brings his foot to his mouth with his left hand.

Barbara: Place the rattle slightly above his head and see if he will grab it.

By using his legs to raise his hips and shift his weight toward his right side, Johan reaches above his head with his left arm and grabs the rattle. He makes jabber noises as he rolls onto his stomach with the toy.

Can you try that again to see if Johan will roll the other way? Johan certainly seems to be a playful boy.

Once again, Johan gracefully initiates a roll from supine to prone by rotating first his head, then his shoulder and hips.

That was beautiful. Can Johan roll from his tummy to his back?

Mother: Yes! He does it all the time. Do you want to see?

Maria: Yes, if you can get him to do it.

Mother attracts Johan's attention with the noisemaker toy. With prompting, Johan rolls from prone to supine. Maria and Barbara notice that he initiates the movement with his head and uses his arms to push off, but he does not rotate his trunk. Once Johan is in supine, Barbara gives Mother two brightly colored 1-inch blocks.

Barbara: Can you get Johan to reach for these?

Mother presents the two blocks to Johan, and he looks from one to the other. He grabs the first block, using a palmar grasp with his right hand.

Try to get him to grab the second block with his left hand.

After Johan grabs the second block, Barbara clutches both of his hands in hers. She brings his hands together in a clapping motion and bangs the two blocks with every musical beat as she sings.

Pat-a-cake, pat-a-cake, baker's man. Bake me a cake as fast as you can.

Barbara lets go of Johan's hands and waits to see if he will continue to bang the blocks as she continues singing. Johan shakes his hands back and forth until one block falls. Barbara stops singing.

Give me the block, Johan.

Johan sits still and stares at Barbara.

Give me the block.

Barbara extends her open hand in front of him as a visual cue.

Give me the block.

Johan moves his hands back and forth. Barbara removes the block from Johan's hand and shows him the noisemaker.

Johan, do you like this noise?

She squeaks the toy, and he smiles. Barbara moves the toy across Johan's field of vision, and he tracks it horizontally and vertically across the midline with smooth ocular control.

Does Johan play on his stomach very much?

Mother: No, not really. But he doesn't mind being on his tummy.

Maria turns Johan to prone. She places the rattle and noisemaker in front of Johan as he props himself on his forearms and looks at the toys that lie just beyond his arms. As soon as Maria squeezes the noisemaker toy, he fully extends his arms to elevate his body and holds this position for almost 10 seconds. Barbara notices that his hands do not fist. Johan turns to look at his mother, kicks his legs in excitement, and squeals. Mother tickles her son as he continues to giggle.

Maria: Here, Johan!

Maria shakes the rattle and squeezes the noisemaker in front of Johan. He takes the noisemaker with his right arm and brings it to his mouth. After a few moments, Maria retrieves the toy and places it under a towel in front of Johan. He moves the towel to retrieve the toy and brings it to his mouth. Barbara places the toy 3 feet in front of Johan, but he does not pull himself forward more than 1 foot to retrieve the toy. He uses a crawling motion and relies heavily on his right arm strength.

Barbara: Does Johan propel himself forward on the floor very far?

Mother: No.

Barbara places a toy attached to a string in front of Johan. He reaches for the string, pulls the toy toward him, and rolls onto his back to look for his mother. Once again, Mother tickles her son, and he smiles.

Maria: I would like to see if Johan will do some more things for me while lying on his stomach. Can you lay him on the floor so that he faces away from you?

Mother: Okay.

Mother places her son in prone position with his feet toward her.

Maria: Now, encourage Johan to turn around on his belly and look at you. Use the toys to encourage him if you would like.

After two attempts, Johan completes this challenge.

Does Johan get into this position?

Maria demonstrates a four-point position.

Mother: He will get into a crawling position with his bottom in the air and sleep that way, but he doesn't crawl.

Maria: Can you place Johan in that position and give him a little help to see what he does?

Mother: I'll try.

Mother has a very difficult time supporting Johan's weight and squirming body. Maria demonstrates by placing one hand under Johan's stomach and positions his legs with her other hand. Mother tries again. Johan fusses, and Mother stops. Johan rolls onto his back, points to Maria's bag of toys, and babbles.

Maria: I would like to put Johan in a sitting position. I'm going to help him by pulling him up with his arms.

Johan tucks his chin, contracts his abdominal muscles, and flexes his legs as he tries to assist. Once sitting in a long-leg position, Maria slowly lets Johan balance himself as she places his hands on the floor in front of him. Johan briefly bears weight through his arms, then shifts his weight posteriorly, places his hands on his thighs, extends his spine slightly, and holds his head upright. Johan sits on his own for approximately 30 seconds before losing his balance. Maria begins to wind up a musical radio and catches Johan's attention, while Barbara places him in a sitting position on the floor.

Figure 3.1 Johan with Radio

Maria: Barbara, can you get him to reach for the radio?

Johan uses protective extension of his arms sideways to catch his balance while reaching but does not appear to have this reflex posteriorly. Maria is able to coax Johan to grab the radio, and he sits alone without his arms for support for approximately 20 seconds. Barbara places the radio in front of Johan. He makes cooing noises and shakes his head and trunk. The adults laugh at his attempt to dance, and Johan giggles.

I would like to stand Johan up. Would you hold the radio up for him and give him some encouragement?

Maria grabs Johan around the upper chest from behind. She lowers his legs onto the floor and encourages him to bear weight through his feet. Johan extends his neck and spine, stands with his knees slightly bent, and squeals to his mother in an attempt to get her attention. Mother laughs.

Mother: Johan, you are standing. That's my boy.

As mother and son continue to converse, Maria encourages Johan to extend his hips and knees so that he can maintain some trunk stability, but she is unsuccessful. Next, Maria holds Johan under his trunk in a suspended prone position. Johan is able to hold his head up and extend his legs independently. As she lowers him to the floor, Johan extends his arms.

Barbara: It appears as though Johan is starting to talk. What kind of noises or words does he try to say?

Mother: He doesn't say "mama" yet, but he says something like "baba." He likes to imitate sounds and noises that I make. He also understands his own name, I think.

Barbara: Very good.

Johan sits on the floor with his noisemaker in his hand and smiles.

The therapists continue for another 5 minutes, primarily talking to Mother about their observations. Although Maria and Barbara are able to share their first impressions, they plan to phone Mother the next day. The therapists want to discuss their findings with other members of the early intervention team and with Dr. Lu. Eventually, Mother and the team will decide if this family qualifies for any of the services ABC-ITP offers.

The Challenge

Assume that you are Barbara. Analyze your observations and decide whether Johan and his mother would benefit from early intervention. As an occupational therapist, do they require your services? If you would like assistance with this challenge, use the questions and resources below to aid your analysis. At a minimum, complete questions 1, 4, 6, 11, and 12. See Appendix E for Selected Answers.

Questions to Aid Analysis

1. What factors may negatively influence infant health during the prenatal, perinatal, and postnatal periods? Could any of these factors influence Johan's health and development?

2. Barbara received the referral for Johan because he was considered at risk. In which risk categories would you place him?

3. What skills and abilities do infants develop in the first 6 months of life? Can you classify these abilities into occupational performance areas (e.g., self-care and play/leisure) and performance components and contexts (e.g., social and emotional development, communication skills, cognitive development, physical development and environment)?

4. Mother and Johan have been followed by a Well Baby Center. What types of services do you think are provided at this clinic? These are services that you will not want to replicate.

5. Describe the developmental stage of infancy according to Erik Erikson, Arnold Gesell, Jean Piaget, and Robert Havighurst. What do these theorists say about sensorimotor, cognitive, communication, social-emotional, and self-help skill development at Johan's stage of development?

6. The observational information contained within this case has been designed to enable you to use the developmental information contained within the *Alberta Infant Motor Scales* (AIMS) (Piper and Darrah 1994), the *Hawaii Early Learning Profile–Revised* (HELP–R) (Furuno and O'Reilly et al. 1988), and the *Peabody Developmental Motor Scales* (PDMS) (Folio and Fewell 1983) to aid and enrich your analysis. This process will enable you to become familiar with these instruments. Will you use Johan's chronological or corrected age?

Formal training, practice apprenticeships, and qualified peer reviews are required for test administration and interpretation competency.

	Month	Day
Chronological Age	5	65
minus Days Premature		?
Corrected Age	?	?

Days premature = (40 weeks – gestation age in weeks) multiplied by 7
Chronological age = 7 months 5 days

7. Infant neuromotor assessments typically evaluate primitive reflex integration, quality of movement performance, and motor milestone achievement. Which approaches do the AIMS, HELP–R, and PDMS use to screen infants? Are there other tests that could be used to evaluate Johan's motor, cognitive, communication, social-emotional, and self-help skills or Mother's parenting needs? (See Appendix A.)

8. Gilfoyle, Grady, and Moore's (1990) theory of spatiotemporal adaptation views the sensory-motor-sensory process as a spiral-shaped continuum. The four components of the adaptive process include assimilation, accommodation, association, and differentiation. A number of principles govern the direction of the spiraling continuum. Describe these principles and use examples from within this case to illustrate the components and principles of this theory.

9. The traditional neuromaturational model of development proposes that motor competencies reflect the maturation of the central nervous system. Piper and Darrah (1994) suggest that this model assumes

   - movement progresses from primitive, mass movement reflex patterns to voluntary, controlled movement;
   - motor development progresses in a cephalo-caudal direction;
   - movement is first controlled proximally, then distally; and
   - motor development is sequential, consistent, and predictable.

   Find evidence within the case to demonstrate how the neuromaturational model has guided Maria and Barbara's evaluation. Specifically, which reflexes did Barbara and Maria test? What evidence is there from Johan's natural play that suggests integration of various primitive reflexes?

10. The contemporary approach to motor control theory borrows from developmental psychology and systems theory (Piper and Darrah 1994). Contentions of this model are

   - a multiplicity of factors contribute to behavior and exert an influence on motoric outcome,
   - motor behaviors are a product of all contributing subsystems,
   - movements are influenced by the task,
   - systems exhibit self-organizing and autonomous properties, and
   - subsystems may develop asynchronously (Piper and Darrah 1994).

   Find evidence in the case to demonstrate how the motor control model has guided Maria's and Barbara's assessment of relevant subsystems, the environment, and the task.

11. Reflect on your answers to questions 4 through 10. Do Johan's occupational performance competencies and performance component skills and abilities vary from the norm? How does his environment impact or have potential to impact on his development?

12. Does this family require early intervention or any type of follow-up service? Explain the reasoning and rationale behind your decision.

13. Assume that you have decided to provide service. What are your long-term goals and short-term objectives? How do you expect to receive funding for your services?

14. Assume that you have decided not to provide service. Does Johan continue to be at risk? Is there any research in the current literature that would assist you in making this decision?

New Terminology

Alberta Infant Motor Scale (AIMS)
Apgar score
at risk
biological risk
cerebral palsy (CP)
chronological age
corrected age
environmental risk

established risk
extremely low birth weight
gestational age
Hawaii Early Learning Profile-Revised (HELP-R)
IFSP
landau
low birth weight
palmar grasp

plasticity
Peabody Developmental Motor Scales (PDMS)
P.L. 99–457
P.L. 101–476
preterm
protective extension
very low birth weight
Well Baby Center

Learning Resources

Information on the AIMS, HELP-R, and the PDMS is provided in Appendix A. Information on accessing Public Law and House Reports is available in Appendix B. Canadian readers should use the uniform terminology proposed in the Client-Centred Model of Occupational Performance in Appendix C.

American Occupational Therapy Association. 1994. Uniform terminology for occupational therapy: Application to practice. 3d ed. *American Journal of Occupational Therapy* 48:1047–59.

American Occupational Therapy Association. 1995. Statement: Reauthorization of the *Individuals with Disabilities Education Act. OT Week* 9:35–38.

Bly, L. 1994. *Motor skills acquisition in the first year: An illustrated guide to normal development.* Tucson, AZ: Therapy Skill Builders.

Case-Smith, J. 1993. *Pediatric occupational therapy and early intervention.* Stoneham, MA: Andover Medical Publishers.

Gilfoyle, E. M., A. P. Grady, and J. C. Moore. 1990. *Children adapt: A theory of sensorimotor-sensory development.* 2d ed. Thorofare, NJ: Slack.

Goudy, K., and J. Fetzer. 1988. *Infant motor development: A look at the phases.* Tucson, AZ: Therapy Skill Builders.

Piper, M. C., and J. Darrah. 1994. Theories of motor development. In *Motor assessment of the developing infant.* Philadelphia: W. B. Saunders.

Sher, B. 1992. *Extraordinary play with ordinary things.* Tucson, AZ: Therapy Skill Builders.

Telepool. *The baby at six months.* Princeton, NJ: Films for the Humanities and Sciences.

U.S. House of Representatives. 1986. *Education of the Handicapped Amendments,* Part H, Public Law 99–457. Washington, D.C.

U.S. House of Representatives. 1990. *Individuals with Disabilities Education Act,* P. L. 101–476. Washington, D.C.

Focus on Research

Escobar, Littenberg, and Petitti (1991) reviewed 111 outcome studies of infants with very low birth weight (less than 1500 grams) and found a median incidence of cerebral palsy (CP) of 7.7% and a median incidence of disability of 25%. In 1993, McCormick, McCarton, Tonascia, and Brooks-Gunn found CP in 10% of their sample of 256 infants with very low birth weight (less than 1500 grams). The population prevalence of CP was 2 per 1000 live births (Rosen and Dickinson 1992). Two epidemiology studies found a history of preterm delivery or small for gestation age in about 40% of children with CP and the presence of both risk factors in almost 25% (Nelson and Ellenberg 1978; Hagberg et al. 1989).

The Infant Health and Development Program was a randomized, controlled longitudinal research study conducted in the United States to determine the efficacy of combining early child development, home visits, parent support groups, systematic educational programs, and family support services (intervention group) with pediatric follow-up (intervention and control groups) offered in the first three years to reduce the incidence of health and development problems in preterm infants with low birth weight at eight medical school sites (Ramey et al. 1992). The intervention group included 377 families; whereas, the control group included 608 families.

Various researchers analyzed the outcome data and determined the following:

> For three-year-olds who had low birth weight as infants, the level of family participation in early intervention is positively correlated with the child's cognitive development (Ramey et al. 1992).

> In infants with low birth weight, intensive intervention increases the intellectual performance of three-year-olds. However, the early intervention does not eliminate other risk factors that are unique for each individual (e.g., sociocultural, psychological, genetic) (Ramey et al. 1992, 464).

> Early intervention improves cognitive performance but does not completely offset the influence of biological and socioeconomic risk of infants with very low birth weight (McCormick et al. 1993).

> In terms of their intellectual outcome at three years, children whose mothers have a high school education or less benefit more from intervention than children whose mothers who have a higher educational level (Brooks-Gunn et al. 1992).

> Significant intervention effects were seen in children's cognitive scores at 24 and 36 months of age, but not at 12 months of age (Brooks-Gunn et al. 1993).

> Significant intervention effects were seen in children's behavior problem scores at 24 and 36 months of age (Brooks-Gunn et al. 1993).

Family income and poverty status are powerful correlates of the cognitive development and behavior of these children. The duration of poverty is significant, but its timing in early childhood is not (Duncan et al. 1994).

Maternal age is not significantly related to child development at 36 months, but co-residency with the infant's grandmother is associated with improved cognitive and health outcomes (Pope et al. 1993).

Mothers who received intervention services were employed for more months and returned to the work force earlier. Future fertility and maternal education were not associated with early intervention (Brooks-Gunn et al. 1994).

References

Brooks-Gunn, J., R. T. Gross, H. C. Kraemer, D. Spiker, and S. Shapiro. 1992. Enhancing the cognitive outcomes of low birth weight, premature infants: For whom is the intervention most effective? Part 2. *Pediatrics* 89:1209–15.

Brooks-Gunn, J., P. K. Klebanov, F. Liaw, and D. Spiker. 1993. Enhancing the development of low birth weight, premature infants: Changes in cognition and behavior over the first three years. *Child Development* 64:736–53.

Brooks-Gunn, J., M. C. McCormick, S. Shapiro, A. Benasich, and G. W. Black. 1994. The effects of early education intervention on maternal employment, public assistance, and health insurance: The infant health and development program. *American Journal of Public Health* 84:924–31.

Cook, D. 1993. Screening and identification in early intervention. In *Pediatric occupational therapy and early intervention,* by J. Case-Smith. Stoneham, MA: Andover Medical Publishers.

Duncan, G. J., J. Brooks-Gunn, and P. K. Klebanov. 1994. Economic deprivation and early childhood development. *Child Development* 65:296–318.

Escobar, G. J., B. Littenberg, and D. B. Petitti. 1991. Outcome among surviving very low birth weight infants: A meta-analysis. *Archives of Disease in Childhood* 66 (February):204–11.

Hagberg, B., G. Hagberg, and R. Zetterstom. 1989. Decreasing perinatal mortality: Increase in cerebral palsy morbidity. *Acta Paediatria Scandinavica* 78:664–70.

McCormick, M. C., C. McCarton, J. Tonascia, and J. Brooks-Gunn. 1993. Early educational intervention for very low birth weight infants: Results from the Infant Health and Development Program. *Journal of Pediatrics* 123:527–33.

Miller, L. J., and G. H. Roid. 1994. *The T.I.M.E. toddler and infant motor evaluation: A standardized assessment.* Tucson, AZ: Therapy Skill Builders.

Nelson, K. B., and J. H. Ellenberg. 1978. Epidemiology of cerebral palsy. *Advances in Neurology* 19:421–35.

Paban, M., and M. C. Piper. 1987. Early predictors of one year neurodevelopmental outcome for at-risk infants. *Physical and Occupational Therapy in Pediatrics* 7:17–34.

Pelletier Sehnal, J., and A. Palmeri. 1989. High-risk infants. In *Occupational therapy for children,* by P. N. Pratt and A. S. Allen, 361–81. St. Louis: C. V. Mosby.

Piper, M. C., and J. Darrah. 1994. *Motor assessment of the developing infant.* Philadelphia: W. B. Saunders.

Pope, S. K., L. Whiteside, J. Brooks-Gunn, K. J. Kelleher, V. I. Rickert, R. H. Bradley, and P. H. Casey. 1993. Low birth weight infants born to adolescent mothers: Effects of coresidency with grandmother on child development. *Journal of the American Medical Association* 269:1396–1400.

Ramey, C. T., D. M. Bryan, B. H. Wasik, J. J. Sparling, K. H. Fendt, and L. M. LaVange. 1992. Infant Health and Development Program for low birth weight, premature infants: Program elements, family participation, and child intelligence. *Pediatrics* 89:454–65.

Rosen, M. G., and J. C. Dickinson. 1992. The incidence of cerebral palsy. *American Journal of Obstetrics and Gynecology* 167:417–23.

U.S. House of Representatives. 1986. *Education of the Handicapped Amendments,* Part H, Public Law 99–457. Washington, D.C.

U.S. House of Representatives. 1990. *Individuals with Disabilities Education Act,* Public Law 101–476. Washington, D.C.

Kari

Healing is a matter of time, but sometimes
it is also a matter of opportunity. *

—Hippocrates

Background

Kari was born prematurely, weighing 1500 grams. Infant and mother urinalysis for perinatal cocaine exposure was positive. At 2 days of age, Kari demonstrated signs and symptoms of neonatal abstinence syndrome (NAS). She received therapy for the first two months until her mother began missing outpatient appointments. Today, Kari is 7 months, corrected age.

Kari's mother is single, 26 years old, and lives with four friends and two children in a government-subsidized apartment complex. Gary is assigned as Kari's case manager, because he knows Mother through his previous job in the social services department. Mother lost her first and only other child to sudden infant death syndrome (SIDS) 18 months ago.

Therapists visit Kari

Dawn and Gary both work for the Infant and Toddler Program (ABC-ITP). The ITP's mission is to provide comprehensive, transdisciplinary, family-focused early intervention services to enhance the development of infants and toddlers with disabilities within a large, urban community. The importance of early intervention is derived from the belief that services will affect child health and well-being (Ramey et al. 1992) and reduce future educational and institutional costs to society (P.L. 99–457; P.L. 101–476). Pelletier, Sehnal, and Palmeri (1989, 363) postulate that the "nature-nurture controversy, the plasticity of the central nervous system, critical periods, and effects of sensory stimulation and deprivation" support the premise that early experiences affect behavior.

Dawn is a pediatric occupational therapist and will be completing Kari's infant screening in two days. As she begins planning the evaluation, Dawn reflects on this child's birth history and family environment.

---

*Reprinted by permission of the publishers and the Loeb Classical Library from Bartlett, J: *Bartlett's Dictionary of Familiar Quotations, 16th ed.*, translated by W. H. S. Jones. Cambridge, MA: Harvard University Press, 1992.

The Challenge

You are Dawn. Prepare for your screening visit with this family. If you would like assistance with this challenge, use the questions and resources below to aid your analysis.

Questions to Aid Analysis

1. What are the occupational performance and component skills and abilities of a 7-month-old child?

2. What role does performance context play in the development of this child? Does the research literature support your assumptions?

3. Is Kari at risk for developmental challenges, occupational performance difficulties, or health problems?

4. Attitudes and beliefs shape and determine behaviors and our relationships with others. Do you have any personal values that may influence your interaction with Kari and her family? To enhance your understanding of the cultural context of substance-exposed children, review the chapter entitled "Theoretical Approaches to Treatment" within *Working with Substance-Exposed Children: Strategies for Professionals* (Puttkammer 1994).

5. Describe your values and determine whether they reflect the core values and attitudes of occupational therapy practice (American Occupational Therapy Association 1993). Plan your evaluation session to ensure that you establish rapport and a healthy therapeutic relationship with this family.

6. Lawlor and Henderson (1989) found that 68% of the therapists they surveyed worked as part of a team. Multidisciplinary teams were the most common (48%), followed by interdisciplinary teams (28%) and transdisciplinary teams (16%). Describe the differences, advantages, and disadvantages among these different teams.

7. Gary will be conducting the family visit with you. How could you use his background as a social worker and his experience with this family to assist you with your evaluation?

8. Is there a parent questionnaire or infant screening tool that would assist you with collecting data? Refer to Appendix A for some assistance in this area. In preparation for your appointment, familiarize yourself with the administration of these instruments.

9. What information do you want to obtain from Kari and her family? Develop a list of questions for Mother and role model your parent interview.

10. What are the symptoms of NAS? What role would an occupational therapist play with this neonatal client population?

11. Should substance-exposed infants and children be considered at risk (established, biological, or environmental)?

New Terminology

Bayley Scales of Infant Development
drug-exposed
fetal alcohol syndrome (FAS)
immunoassay
in utero
neonatal abstinence syndrome (NAS)
Brazelton Neonatal Behavior
Assessment Scale

placenta
plasticity
prenatal
sudden infant death syndrome (SIDS)
Stanford-Binet Intelligence Scale, 4th ed.
transdisciplinary
very low birth weight
perinatal

Learning Resources

American Occupational Therapy Association. 1993. Core values and attitudes of occupational therapy practice. *American Journal of Occupational Therapy* 47:1085–86.

American Occupational Therapy Association. 1989. Human immunodeficiency virus: Position paper. *American Journal of Occupational Therapy* 43:803–04.

American Occupational Therapy Association. 1994. Uniform terminology for occupational therapy and application to practice. 3d ed. *American Journal of Occupational Therapy* 48:1047–59.

American Occupational Therapy Association. 1994. Occupational therapy code of ethics. *American Journal of Occupational Therapy* 43:1037–38.

Fulks, M. L., and S. R. Harris. 1995. Children exposed to drugs in utero: Their scores on the *Miller Assessment for Preschoolers*. *Canadian Journal of Occupational Therapy* 62:7–15.

Lawlor, M. C., and A. Henderson. 1989. A descriptive study of the clinical practice patterns of occupational therapists working with infants and young children. *American Journal of Occupational Therapy* 43:755–64.

Linder, T. W. 1993. *Transdisciplinary play-based assessment*. Baltimore: Paul H. Brookes.

Puttkammer, C. H. 1994. *Working with substance-exposed children: Strategies for professionals*. Tucson, AZ: Therapy Skill Builders.

Richardson, G. A., N. L. Day, and P. J. McGauhey. 1993. The impact of prenatal marijuana and cocaine use on the infant and child. *Clinical Obstetrics and Gynecology* 36:302–18.

Schneider, J. W., and I. J. Chasnoff. 1992. Motor assessment of cocaine/polydrug exposed infants at 4 months. *Neurotoxicology and Teratology* 14:97–101.

U.S. Department of Health and Human Services, Public Health Service. 1992. *Healthy people 2000*. Boston: Jones and Bartlett Publishers.

Focus on Research

It is estimated that 5% to 25% of infants born each year in the United States are exposed in utero to illicit drugs, alcohol, and tobacco (Public Health Service 1992; Vega et al. 1993). The incidence of cocaine-exposed infants has been estimated to range from 8% to 17% (Richardson et al. 1993). Fetal alcohol syndrome (FAS) affects as many as one to three infants per 1,000 live births nationally (National Center for Health Statistics 1990). SIDS is the leading cause of infant mortality after the first month of life. Although the causes of SIDS are unknown, risk factors include maternal smoking and drug use and infants born to families with a history of SIDS (Public Health Service 1992).

Cocaine and multiple drug exposure can have significant direct and indirect effects on development, likely secondary to

- intrauterine growth retardation and small head circumference (Fomufod 1994; Griffith et al. 1994),
- impaired placental blood flow causing hypoxia (Woods et al. 1987),
- low and very low birth weight (Harsham et al. 1994; Chasnoff et al. 1992),
- prematurity (Fomufod 1994),
- inadequate prenatal care and an impoverished social environment (Richardson et al. 1993).

Although substance exposure does not affect all infants equally, some of these children

- demonstrate depressed interactive abilities and poor state control when tested on the *Brazelton Neonatal Behavioral Assessment Scale* (Chasnoff et al. 1985),
- perform one standard deviation below the mean on the *Bayley Scales of Infant Development* at 6, 12, and 24 months (Chasnoff et al. 1992),
- obtain lower sensory processing and language performance on the *Miller Assessment of Preschoolers* (Fulks and Harris 1995),
- demonstrate poor verbal reasoning at 3 years on the *Stanford-Binet Intelligence Scale,* 4th ed.(Griffith et al. 1994), and
- may do well in highly structured, nurturing, fully integrated educational environments (Powell 1994).

Cocaine and poly-drug exposed infants are 40 times more likely to experience developmental motor delays at age 4 months, as measured by the *Movement Assessment of Infants* (Schneider and Chasnoff 1992). Cocaine exposure among infants with very low birth weight is associated with a higher incidence of significant cognitive and motor delays by the second year of life, as measured by performance on the *Bayley Scales of Infant Development,* and lower levels of sustained attention, interest in objects, and play behavior than matched peers (Singer et al. 1994).

Cocaine-using mothers tend to be older, unmarried, and are more likely to also use alcohol, marijuana, and tobacco during their pregnancy. They typically receive limited prenatal care and are of lower socioeconomic status (Day et al. 1993; Richardson et al. 1993). Cocaine-exposed infants are more likely to live with adoptive families, relatives, or foster care by their second year (Singer et al. 1994).

References

Chasnoff, I. J., W. J. Burns, S. H. Schnoll, and K. A. Burns. 1985. Cocaine use in pregnancy. *New England Journal of Medicine* 313:666–69.

Chasnoff, I. J., D. R. Griffith, C. Freier, and J. Murray. 1992. Cocaine/polydrug use in pregnancy: Two-year follow-up. *Pediatrics* 89:284–89.

Day, N. L., C. M. Cottreau, and G. A. Richardson. 1993. The epidemiology of alcohol, marijuana, and cocaine use among women of childbearing age and pregnant women. *Clinical Obstetrics and Gynecology* 36:232–45.

Fomufod, A. K. 1994. The substance-abusing pregnant woman. In *Working with substance-exposed children: Strategies for professionals,* edited by C. H. Puttkammer. Tucson, AZ: Therapy Skill Builders.

Fulks, M. L., and S. R. Harris. 1995. Children exposed to drugs in utero: Their scores on the *Miller Assessment for Preschoolers. Canadian Journal of Occupational Therapy* 62:7–15.

Griffith, D. R., S. D. Azuma, and I. J. Chasnoff. 1994. Three-year outcome of children exposed prenatally to drugs. *Journal of the American Academy of Adolescent Psychiatry* 33:20–27.

Harsham, J., J. H. Keller, and D. Disbrow. 1994. Growth patterns of infants exposed to cocaine and other drugs in utero. *Journal of the American Dietetic Association* 94:999–1007.

National Center for Health Statistics. 1990. *Health, United States, 1989 and prevention profile.* DHHS Pub. No. (PHS)90–1232. Hyattsville, MD: U.S. Department of Health and Human Services.

Pelletier Sehnal, J., and A. Palmeri. 1989. High-risk infants. In *Occupational therapy for children,* by P. N. Pratt and A. S. Allen, 361–81. St. Louis: C. V. Mosby.

Powell, D. 1994. Educational interventions for substance-exposed children now in preschool and kindergarten. In *Working with substance-exposed children: Strategies for professionals,* edited by C. H. Puttkammer. Tucson, AZ: Therapy Skill Builders.

Public Health Service. U.S. Department of Health and Human Services. 1992. *Healthy people 2000.* Boston: Jones and Bartlett Publishers.

Ramey, C. T., D. M. Bryan, B. H. Wasik, J. J. Sparling, K. H. Fendt, and L. M. LaVange. 1992. Infant health and development program for low birth weight, premature infants: Program elements, family participation, and child intelligence. *Pediatrics* 89:454–65.

Richardson, G. A., N. L. Day, and P. J. McGauhey. 1993. The impact of prenatal marijuana and cocaine use on the infant and child. *Clinical Obstetrics and Gynecology* 36:302–18.

Schneider, J. W., and I. J. Chasnoff. 1992. Motor assessment of cocaine/polydrug exposed infants at age 4 months. *Neurotoxicology and Teratology* 14:97–101.

Singer, L. T., T. S. Yamashita, S. Hawkins, D. Cairns, J. Baley, and R. Kliegman. 1994. Increased incidence of intraventricular hemorrhage and developmental delay in cocaine-exposed, very low birth weight infants. Part 2. *Journal of Pediatrics* 124:765–71.

U.S. House of Representatives. 1986. *Education of the Handicapped Amendments, Part H, Public Law 99–457*. Washington, D.C.

U.S. House of Representatives. 1990. *Individuals with Disabilities Education Act, Public Law 101–476*. Washington, D.C.

Vega, W. A., B. Kolody, J. Hwang, and A. Noble. 1993. Prevalence and magnitude of perinatal substance exposure in California. *New England Journal of Medicine* 329:850–54.

Woods, J. R., M. A. Plessinger, and K. E. Clerk. 1987. Effect of cocaine on uterine blood flow and fetal oxygenation. *Journal of the American Medical Association* 257:957–61.

Antonio

*The splendor of infancy is perhaps best expressed and
celebrated by observing the infant explore and discover
the world through the development of movement.* *

—Piper and Darrah

Background

While reviewing the Infant and Family Performance Profile screening report, Terry
reflected on the first time that he met Antonio and his mother just over a year ago. At
that time, Terry worked at a local pediatric hospital and received a referral and pre-
scription to fabricate a wrist splint for a newborn. Antonio and his mother arrived for
their appointment late and sat quietly throughout most of the session. While Terry
was busy designing the smallest hand splint he had ever made, Antonio's mother had
tears in her eyes. Antonio's parents had just been informed by Dr. Jackson that "Antonio had brain damage . . . cerebral palsy." Cerebral palsy (CP) results more com-
monly from prenatal abnormalities than from perinatal difficulties (Eicher and Batshaw
1993), and the presence of Antonio's contracture at birth suggested a prenatal insult.
Antonio was hungry and crying. A tear rolled down his cheek as he started to breast
feed. Mother and son cried together.

Therapist visits Antonio

One year later, Terry works for the Infant and Family Program (IFP). Together with
two other early intervention professionals, Terry is completing an evaluation of the
family's progress. The team members have completed their screening and are beginning a more thorough evaluation. They are scheduled to meet with the family to
discuss their findings. Terry reflects on the interview with the family and the information that the team has collected on the Infant and Family Performance Profile to
determine whether occupational therapy services are needed.

The IFP uses an interdisciplinary team model to provide a home-based, family-focused approach to early intervention. The goal of early intervention is to empower
parents and families to facilitate the growth and development of their child with special needs and to effectively use coping strategies to find satisfaction in their roles as
providers and caregivers (American Occupational Therapy Association 1988). The
IFP provides services to children from birth to 2 years, as outlined in the Education of
the Handicapped Amendments of 1986 (P.L. 99–457, Part H) and amended in the
Individuals with Disabilities Education Act of 1990 (P.L. 101–476). (See Appendix B

---

*Piper, M., and J. Darrah. 1994. *Motor Assessment of the Developing Infant.* Philadelphia:
W. B. Saunders. Reprinted with permission from author and publisher.

for details.) Home-based intervention enables therapists to acquire realistic and relevant information about the child's cultural, social, and physical environment. Parents, when visited at home, show a higher degree of involvement and less parental stress. This benefit is balanced with the requirement that therapists be flexible and creative (Hinojosa et al. 1988).

Infant and Family Performance Profile

Child's name: *Antonio*   Therapist's name: *Terry*   Date: *January 9*

I. Introduction
Between the age of 1 and 2 months, Antonio received OT services from this therapist at ABC Children's Hospital. This current evaluation was completed on January 7 and 8, following the receipt of a referral from Dr. Jackson, Antonio's pediatrician, on January 3 for a developmental follow-up. No other service agency is involved at this time.

II. Assessment
Data were compiled from an interview with Antonio's father and four-year-old sister Rosa, a structured play observation, a performance checklist, and a neurological screening. Antonio's chronological age is 16 months, but he was born 1 month premature.

A. Parent Resources and Identified Concerns
Although Antonio's mother was not available for this interview, his father and sister identified a number of concerns regarding his health and well-being. The *Canadian Occupational Performance Measure* (COPM) (Law, Baptiste, Carswell, McColl, Polatajko, and Pollock 1994) was used to identify the five most important developmental issues.

Antonio's father and sister rank ordered (1-10) these concerns according to the following criteria:
Importance: How important it is for Antonio to do the activity?
Performance: How well does Antonio perform the activity?
Satisfaction: How satisfied is the family with the way Antonio currently performs the activity?

A ranking of 10 corresponds to extremely important, able to do it extremely well, and extremely satisfied with the way the activity is performed. A ranking of 1 corresponds to not important at all, not able to do it, and not satisfied at all. (Law et al. 1994, Canadian Occupational Performance Measure, 2d ed. Toronto: Canadian Occupational Therapy Association.)

Table 3.2 Performance Measure

	Important	Performance	Satisfaction
"Antonio is unsafe sitting in the bathtub."	10	4	2
"Antonio cannot walk by himself."	8	1	1
"Antonio doesn't use his left hand to play."	8	3	3
"Antonio doesn't talk much."	6	2	3
"Rosa and Antonio don't play together."	7	5	1

Reprinted by permission from Canadian Occupational Therapy Association. Law et al. 1994, *Canadian Occupational Performance Measure*, 2d ed. Toronto.

Before both IFP appointments, Antonio's mother was called in to work at the last minute. She promised to be present during the next IFP visit. Antonio's father indicates that Antonio's mother is concerned that her son does not walk or talk, and she wonders whether the therapists know of any other Spanish-speaking families with children who have cerebral palsy. She wants to know if they are confusing Antonio by speaking to him in English and Spanish. Father indicates that both he and his wife are coping well and are only concerned that they cannot do anything to help Antonio move better.

B. Adaptive Functioning

Self-Care. Antonio feeds himself liquids from a cup with his right hand. He uses a spoon for purée and soft chunky foods but frequently spills. He enjoys eating very small pieces of tortilla and banana on his own but refuses to take other solid foods. Father did not express any concerns regarding Antonio's current feeding or nutritional status.

By his father's description, Antonio sits independently with his legs wide apart but frequently loses his balance backward or toward the left. He will not reach out with his left hand to catch himself when he falls toward this side.

Antonio is bathed in the bathtub with close supervision. He "dislikes bath time and having his teeth brushed. He cries the entire time. He likes to dry his own body after a bath and doesn't seem to want help." When asked whether Antonio understands the function of a hairbrush, Father replies, "Yes, he likes to help by holding onto the handle but generally just doesn't like having his hair brushed or combed." Antonio remains in diapers. During the assessment, he blew his nose into a tissue with assistance.

Antonio's father reports that Antonio assists with upper body dressing by raising his right arm, and kicks his feet to help with removing his pants. Rosa reports that "Antonio hates socks and shoes. He cries when they are put on and always pulls them off himself." Antonio is able to remove loose pants with effort but is unable to remove his shirt or put any garments on himself. He has a regular car seat, but his father indicates that he cries the entire time during car rides and occasionally vomits in the car.

Play and Leisure. Antonio is able to transition from a sitting position to four-point (creeping) position, which he maintains for a few minutes. In quadruped, his left hand fists, and he collapses occasionally on his left support arm. He does not rock forward or backward in this position. Antonio crawls forward 3 feet with encouragement and minimal trunk support. Antonio rolls toward both directions as his primary means of locomotion. Mother is apparently very pleased with this newest development, but father expresses concern that Antonio's actions are hazardous. "Antonio can make his way to the door and push it open. We have to be careful. He hasn't mastered stairs, but I'm sure that will be next."

In supine, Antonio plays with a toy with his hands together but does not spontaneously touch his knees or legs from this position or independently rise to a sitting position. When his tummy is tickled in supine, Antonio begins to scream and his left lower extremity extends and his left hand fists. Antonio plays in prone on his elbows with bilateral forearm weight bearing. From this position, he will reach for an image of himself in a mirror with his right arm and occasionally will spontaneously extend his arms to raise his trunk. No pivot prone extension is seen.

Antonio does not pull to stand but takes many steps in standing when supported at chest level. He is not able to control his descent from standing and relies on external support for these transitional movements. Antonio will not cruise while hanging onto furniture, even after prompting, and he does not appear to enjoy being moved, rocked, or bounced by his parents or me.

When Antonio sits, his spine is usually slightly rounded, and his left leg is flexed. He will lean forward and rotate his body to reach for a favorite toy and pivot toward his right to retrieve a toy placed behind him. While sitting, he will use his right hand and leg to scoot himself forward a few feet to retrieve his toy piano. When his legs are straightened to a long-leg sit, he holds the position for only a few minutes. Antonio's right arm shows accurate reach with a pincer grasp. He uses his extended right index finger as a pointer for exploring small openings and playing his piano. He is able to turn thick pages of a children's book with his right hand and looks at the pictures momentarily. Antonio places three 1-inch blocks in a cup but cannot stack them on top of each other on a flat surface. During strenuous or challenging activities, Antonio tends to hold his left hand flexed (thumb in hand) with the humerus slightly abducted, forearm pronated, and elbow and wrist flexed. Antonio moves in and out of this high-guard position.

Antonio is fond of noisemakers, his toy piano, rattles, and large blocks. He likes to shake toys and can remove three large pegs from a board and two rings from a stand before deliberately dropping them on the floor from his high chair. He looks to the floor to find the dropped peg or ring. He occasionally startles in response to very loud noises and dislikes coarsely textured toys. Antonio uses a pincer (two-point pinch) grasp to obtain small pieces of tortilla placed on the table in front of him.

Father indicates that Rosa, his sister, tends to avoid playing with Antonio, and she describes him as a "cry baby" who puts everything in his mouth and just likes to bang things. When given two 1-inch blocks, Antonio bangs them together and giggles. He uses a left radial palmar and right pincer grasp.

C. Performance Components and Contexts that Affect Daily Living

Social/Emotional Development. Antonio waves good-bye at the end of our session. Rosa indicates that he recognizes the whole family and some of the neighborhood kids. Antonio watches his sister play and appears to enjoy her proximity. Rosa enjoys playing Pat-a-Cake with her brother because he giggles throughout the game.

Communication Skills. Antonio communicates with his sister with vocalizations and will occasionally share or show off a new toy. Antonio responds to his name by looking and smiling, replies to a "no-no" command by stopping and looking around, and reacts appropriately when asked, "Can you give it to me?" His receptive vocabulary appears much greater than his expressive vocabulary. He does not vocalize often but uses words that approximate names; for instance, "ma" (madre), "pa" (padre), and "a" (Rosa).

Cognitive Development. Antonio seeks and obtains his favorite toys when they are hidden from view. He is very watchful of surroundings and becomes anxious when separated from his father. He is able to attend to purposeful activities for several minutes and spends time watching and smiling as his sister engages in pretend play. Antonio's father describes him as very structured and notes that Antonio does not like it when his routine is changed.

Physical Development. Antonio's father is not concerned about his vision or hearing. To his knowledge, Antonio has not been assessed in these areas. There is evidence of asymmetric tonic neck reflex (ATNR), but the Moro and rooting reflexes are integrated. He has a positive Babinski on the left side. His legs extend when he pulls to sit. Anterior and right lateral protective reactions are present. Protective extension to the left and posterior are absent. Trunk righting reactions are evident on the right side. Equilibrium reactions in sitting are immature.

Antonio has mild resistance to quick stretch at the end ranges of left knee extension, dorsiflexion, forearm supination, and wrist extension. He appears to have pain or discomfort on the left forearm in supination. He has full passive range of motion (PROM), no clonus, and no obvious arm length discrepancy. He has a mobile spine with a tendency for lateral left flexion seen in pronation and sitting.

Environment. Antonio lives in a small apartment with his parents and sister. Father works full-time as a salesman, and mother works four days a week as a short-order cook. While their parents work, the children stay with their extended family who live in the same apartment complex. Antonio's grandparents care for the children most days and do not speak English. During the home visit, Father frequently spoke about cousins, aunts, uncles, and grandparents and how they love having a baby around. This family speaks Spanish in the home, although both parents and Rosa are fluent in English. The family has a number of stimulating toys and appears to provide many childhood play opportunities for their children.

III. Interpretation

Antonio, a 16-month-old boy who received a diagnosis of cerebral palsy at age 1 month, was screened by an occupational therapist (OT) at the request of Dr. Jackson. Although his social skills appear to be within age range, his feeding and play skills are slow in developing. His feeding skills are typical of a 9-month-old and are characterized by oral motor incoordination and sensory sensitivities. His gross motor competencies and play skills are equally delayed and are likely influenced by his hypotonic trunk, spastic extremities, and delayed development of postural control. His gross and fine motor skills are asymmetrical and likely affected by tactile and vestibular sensitivities, poor left cocontraction, and proximal instability. His parents appear eager to see him succeed. The quantity and quality of sibling interaction should be assessed further.

Figure 3.2 Antonio with Piano

The Challenge

You are Terry. In anticipation of a meeting with your colleagues and Antonio's parents, piece together all of the data you have collected to decide if Antonio needs occupational therapy. If you would like assistance with this challenge, use the following questions and resources to aid your analysis. At a minimum, complete questions 1 through 8. See Selected Answers in Appendix E.

Questions to Aid Analysis

1. How does screening differ from evaluation? Why is it conducted before an evaluation?

2. What are the self-care, play, and leisure competencies of a 16-month-old child?

3. Now that you have begun Antonio's evaluation, what is your opinion about how his competencies compare to the norm?

The observational information contained within this case has been designed to enable you to use the developmental milestone information contained within the *Denver II,* the *Hawaii Early Learning Profile-Revised* (HELP-R), and the *Peabody Developmental Motor Scales* (PDMS) to aid and enrich your analysis. Which test items would you need to perform to complete and score these tests? Will you use Antonio's chronological or corrected age? This process will enable you to become familiar with these instruments. *Formal training, practice apprenticeship, and qualified peer reviews are required for test administration competency.*

4. List some of the prenatal, perinatal, and postnatal causes of cerebral palsy (CP) and review the classification systems used to describe the various types of CP. From your clinical observations of Antonio, how would you classify his CP? What are the characteristics of spasticity? Hypotonia? Do you consider Antonio to be at risk (established, biological, or environmental)?

5. What do you think of the family's perceptions of Antonio? Do you have answers to his mother's questions? How does the family's identified issues compare to your own?

6. Complete the chart on page 52 by delineating both the family's and your concerns regarding Antonio's performance, the performance components and contexts that affect them, and some behavioral observations supporting these claims. The *Uniform Terminology for Occupational Therapy* document from the American Occupational Therapy Association (1994) provides a taxonomy system that will assist you in this process. By documenting behavioral evidence, you can more easily define measurable and objective outcome indicators. The chart has been started for you.

7. Given the information the team has compiled to date, what occupational performance problems are evident, and what are your goals as an OT? Ensure that your goals maintain or promote function and prevent dysfunction as well as fit the concerns, priorities, and resources of this family. Be prepared to modify these recommendations after discussing them with Antonio's parents and your team. Complete the outline of goals on page 53.

Problem 1: Antonio is unable to sit safely in the tub due to delayed reflex development, postural control, and left lower extremity spasticity.

Goal 1: Antonio will sit independently and safely in the tub using adaptive equipment by February 1.

Performance Areas Concern	Contributory Performance Components and Context	Supporting Behavioral Observations
Self-Care *Unable to safely sit in the tub.*	**Sensorimotor** *Delayed reflex development, postural control, and left lower extremity spasticity.*	*No left protective extension.*
	Cognitive	
	Psychological	
Play and Leisure		
	Psychosocial	
	Contexts	

Problem 2:

      Goal 2:

Problem 3:

      Goal 3:

Problem 4:

      Goal 4:

Problem 5:

      Goal 5:

8. Antonio's parents have concurred with your recommendations and want you to provide occupational therapy intervention to attain these goals. Would Antonio and his family benefit from direct OT service, monitoring, or consultation? What theoretical frames of reference will you use to determine the focus of your evaluation and subsequent treatment? What assessments could you use to complete your evaluation of Antonio? (Refer to Appendix A for assistance.)

9. In anticipation of meeting with Antonio's parents and your IFP colleagues, write your perceptions of the issues that will need to be addressed in the individual family service plan (IFSP). In the United States, P.L. 99-457 requires that an intervention plan include the following:

> Antonio's "present level of physical development, cognitive development, language and speech development, psychosocial development, and self-help skills, based on acceptable objective criteria (P.L. 99-457)."

> A "statement of the family's strengths and needs relating to enhancing the development" of Antonio (P.L. 99-457).

A statement of the major outcomes expected, including the criteria, procedures, and time lines.

The specific services necessary to meet Antonio's and his family's unique needs, including the frequency, intensity, and the method of service delivery.

Projected dates of service initiation and duration (P.L. 99-457 Sec. 677(d) 1986; see Appendix B).

10. The IFP provides a number of different health and education professional services. Who would be the most appropriate case manager? Why?

11. Antonio's family and the IFP team have agreed to your Goal 1. You have decided to recommend a bath seat. Which model will you recommend? Does the family have equipment funding assistance options?

12. You have had the opportunity to be exposed to the IFP documentation format and style. As an occupational therapist involved in continuous quality improvement (CQI), determine which report-writing strategies you would like to incorporate into your work. Do you have suggestions to improve the IFP's format?

13. Why would Antonio's wrist contracture more likely be secondary to cerebral palsy than a birth trauma, Erb's palsy?

14. The *Individuals with Disabilities Education Act* (P.L. 101–476) was scheduled for reauthorization in September 1995. What was the outcome of this congressional review?

New Terminology

ATNR
brachial plexus
Babinski
cerebral palsy
cohort
COPM
CQI
crawling
creeping
equilibrium reactions
Erb's palsy
HELP-R

hemiplegia
high-guard position
hyperreflexia
IFSP
*Individuals with Disabilities
 Education Act* (IDEA)
PDMS
perinatal
pincer grasp
pivot prone
postnatal
prenatal

preterm
PROM
protective extension
radial-palmar grasp
reciprocal creeping
stepping reflex
stretch reflex
spastic CP
swimming
term
two-point pinch

Learning Resources

Information on the COPM, *Denver II,* HELP-R, and PDMS is provided in Appendix A. Information on accessing Public Law and House Reports is available in Appendix B. Canadian readers should use the uniform terminology proposed in the *Client-Centred Model of Occupational Performance* outlined in Appendix C.

American Occupational Therapy Association. 1988. *Occupational therapy in early intervention and preschool services.* Bethesda, MD.

American Occupational Therapy Association. 1994. Uniform terminology for occupational therapy. 3d ed. *American Journal of Occupational Therapy* 48:1047–54.

Bazyk, S. 1989. Changes in attitudes and beliefs regarding parent participation in home programs: An update. *American Journal of Occupational Therapy* 43:723–28.

Case-Smith J. 1991. Occupational and physical therapists as case managers in early intervention. *Physical and Occupational Therapy in Pediatrics* 11:53–70.

Cech, D., and S. Martin. 1995. *Functional movement development across the life span.* Philadelphia: W. B. Saunders.

Eicher, P. S., and M. L. Batshaw. 1993. Cerebral palsy. *Pediatric Clinics of North America* 40:537–51.

Law, M., S. Baptiste, A. Carswell, M. A. McColl, H. Polatajko, and N. Pollock. 1994. *Canadian Occupational Performance Measure.* 2d ed. Toronto: Canadian Association of Occupational Therapists Publications.

Lynch, E. W., and M. J. Hanson. 1992. *Developing cross-cultural competence: A guide for working with young children and their families.* Baltimore: Paul H. Brookes.

Morris, S. E., and M. D. Klein. 1987. *Pre-feeding skills: A comprehensive resource for feeding development.* Tucson, AZ: Therapy Skill Builders.

U.S. House of Representatives. 1986. *Education of the Handicapped Amendments.* Public Law 99–457. Washington, D.C.

U.S. House of Representatives. 1990. *Individuals with Disabilities Education Act:* Public Law 101–476. Washington, D.C.

Walle, T., and A. Harikainen-Sorri. 1993. Obstetric shoulder injury: Associated risk factors, prediction and prognosis. *Acta Obstetricia et Gynecologica Scandinavica* 72:450–54.

Focus on Research

"Cerebral palsy (CP) refers to a collection of nonprogressive disorders of movement and posture due to an impairment of the immature brain" (Batshaw, Perret, and Kurtz 1992). Central nervous system injury in children who receive a cerebral palsy diagnosis usually occurs in the first 3 to 5 years of life (Eicher and Batshaw 1993). Injury is sustained in utero (44 %), during labor and delivery (19%), at birth (8%), or shortly after birth (5%), but approximately one-quarter (24%) of all cases have no definable cause. In approximately 43% of cases, the diagnosis of CP is made before 6 months of age and in 70% of all cases by 1 year (Eicher and Batshaw 1993). The general population incidence of cerebral palsy in the United States has increased from 2.2 per 1,000 live births in 1980 to 2.3 in 1986 (National Center for Health Statistics 1992). Bhushan and colleagues (1993) attribute this change to the increased proportion of low and very low birth weight infants among children with CP. In 1990, 9.7% of all occupational therapists in the United States indicated cerebral palsy as the most frequent health problem in their clients. This diagnosis ranked third most prevalent, behind cerebral vascular accident (27.1%) and developmentally delayed (12.9%) (American Occupational Therapy Association 1991).

The manifestations and associated deficits of CP include variable impairments in motor, cognitive, sensory, and communicative abilities. Eicher and Batshaw (1993) indicate $2/3$ of the children with cerebral palsy have mental retardation. Approximately 60% of children with hemiplegic cerebral palsy have normal intelligence but demonstrate perceptual impairments that place them at risk for learning disabilities.

References

American Occupational Therapy Association. 1988. Occupational therapy services in early intervention and preschool services. *American Journal of Occupational Therapy* 42:793–94.

American Occupational Therapy Association. 1991. 1990 Membership Data Survey. *OT Week* (22 May):1–8.

American Occupational Therapy Association. 1994. Uniform terminology for occupational therapy. 3d ed. *American Journal of Occupational Therapy* 48:1047–54.

Batshaw, M.L., Y. M. Perret, and L. Kurtz. 1992. Cerebral palsy. In Batshaw, M.L., and Y. M. Perret. *Children with disabilities: A medical primer.* 3d. ed. Baltimore: Paul H. Brookes.

Bhushan, V., N. Paneth, and J. L. Kiely. 1993. Impact of improved survival of very low birth weight infants on recent secular trends in the prevalence of cerebral palsy. *Pediatrics* 91:1094–1100.

Hinojosa, J., J. Anderson, and C. Strauch. 1988. Pediatric occupational therapy in the home. *American Journal of Occupational Therapy* 42:17–22.

Piper, M. C., and J. Darrah. 1994. *Motor assessment of the developing infant*. Philadelphia: W. B. Saunders.

U.S. House of Representatives. 1986. *Education of the handicapped amendments*. Public Law 99–457. Washington, D.C.

U.S. House of Representatives. 1990. *Individuals with disabilities education act*. Public Law 101–476. Washington, D.C.

Module 4

Early Childhood Clinical Cases

	Rozmin	Simon (Part 1)	Simon (Part 2)	Pierre
PBL Approach	Case method	Vignette	Vignette	Case method
Age	18 months	3 years 6 months	3 years 6 months	5 years
Primary Diagnosis	Burn injury	Developmental delay	Developmental delay	Down's syndrome
Area of Practice	Program and discharge planning	Screening	Evaluation	Screening Program planning
Location of Practice	Acute care	Community	Community	Day-care
Frame of Reference	Biomechanical Coping	Developmental Holistic	Developmental Holistic	Behavioral
Performance Area	Activities of daily living (ADL) and Play	Activities of daily living (ADL) Preacademic play	Activities of daily living (ADL) Preacademic play	Activities of daily living (ADL) Preacademic play
Performance Components	Sensorimotor Musculoskeletal Psychosocial Psychological	Sensorimotor Psychosocial Spiritual	Sensorimotor Cognitive Psychosocial Psychological Spiritual	Sensorimotor Cognitive Psychosocial Psychological
Performance Context	Single parent Low income African-American	Reservation Native American	Reservation Native American	Developmental Maturation
Clinical Issues	New therapist Discharge planning	New therapist Cultural context	New therapist Cultural context	Consultation Documentation
Occupational Therapy Tests	Range of Motion	*FirstSTEP*	MAP	Adaptive functioning

Miller Assessment for Preschoolers (MAP); FirstSTEP Screening Tool for Evaluating Preschoolers

Early Childhood Clinical Cases

Rozmin

I will use treatment to help the sick
according to my ability and judgement. *

—Hippocrates

Background

After working for 3 years in outpatient pediatrics, Jan decided that she wanted to transfer to acute care. ABC Medical Center (ABC-MC) offered her a job in its burn unit, and Jan accepted. She was nervous about treating burn patients, but she prepared for this challenging new position by reviewing textbook illustrations and information on burn pathology and treatment.

ABC-MC provides comprehensive, multidisciplinary, rehabilitation services to children and adolescents and has a reputation for excellence in burn care. Burns are the largest cause of accidental death of children in the home (Carvajal 1990) and are classified according to the depth of skin injury and the extent of skin surface involved. Skin surface assessment for adults determines the percentage of total body surface area (TBSA) involved by following the Rule of Nines (Lynch 1979). Infants and children are evaluated using the Rule of Fives to account for different body proportions (Lynch 1979). Classifying burn injuries is important for treatment and prognosis.

Major burns in children include
- twenty-percent TBSA partial-thickness burns,
- more than 10% TBSA full-thickness burns,
- any partial- or full-thickness burn involving more than 5% TBSA in a child less than 2 years of age,
- all burns complicated by other medical problems,
- all inhalation and electrical burns, and
- any burn involving eyes, ears, face, hands, feet, or genitalia

(American Burn Association 1992).

---

*Reprinted by permission of the publishers and the Loeb Classical Library from Bartlett, J: *Bartlett's Dictionary of Familiar Quotations, 16th ed.,* translated by W. H. S. Jones. Cambridge, MA: Harvard University Press, 1992.

ABC-MC's Department of Occupational Therapy

The burn treatment team at ABC-MC includes physicians, dietitians, nurses, occupational and physical therapists, psychologists, and social workers. The role of the occupational therapist in the acute phase management of burns is to prevent dysfunctional positioning and to aid in edema and infection control. Prophylactic use of positioning devices, such as splints, and gentle range of motion (ROM) exercises prevent loss of joint integrity secondary to disuse and edema. Splints are removed two or three times daily for wound cleaning, dressing changes, and exercise. Wound care includes chemical or mechanical debridement and continues until skin restoration and reconstruction is complete. Skin grafts are required for deep burns since spontaneous healing is impossible. Grafting may require that the therapist provide splints to immobilize joints proximal and distal to the site for a minimum of 5 days after surgery (Binder 1992).

The rehabilitative phase begins once wound closure is attained and the patient is medically stable. Occupational therapy intervention continues to focus on maximizing occupational performance potential by minimizing physical deformity, restoring independence or participation in normal life activities, and promoting adjustment. The management of hypertrophic scarring, prevention of contractures, and recovery of strength and ROM is critical to regaining and maintaining function.

Burn splints help maintain soft tissue and joint integrity by aligning the limb or extremity. Splints must conform to body contours to minimize shearing forces on new skin and to avoid pressure sores (Leman 1992). Serial static splints may be used in conjunction with aggressive ROM to maintain increases in joint mobility. Bivalve serial casting is an option for providing circumferential pressure and prolonged stretch to severe contractures (Miles and Grigsby 1990; Ridgeway et al. 1991).

To produce a flat and pliable scar that does not restrict movement, therapists use garments and splints to apply constant, conforming pressure to hypertrophic scar tissue and use splints to maintain joint integrity or to increase ROM (Carr-Collins 1992). Applied after wound closure, garments and splints provide pressure that inhibits scar contracture and hypertrophy, curbs vascular and lymphatic pooling, and averts hypersensitive fragile skin (Miles and Grigsby 1990). Pressure garments are indicated for all donor sites, graft sites, and burn wounds that need more than 10 to 14 days to heal (Deitch et al. 1983). Hypertrophic scar maturation requires 12 to 18 months while keloid scarring requires 2 to 3 years (Salisbury et al. 1990). Keloids occur at a higher incidence in individuals with dark skin and hypertrophic scarring is greater in children than adults (Miles and Grigsby 1990).

According to Carr-Collins, the choice of appropriate contact media is influenced by the injury's size, location, and depth; the scar's tolerance for shear and pressure; the patient's involvement in his or her own rehabilitation; and product availability (Carr-Collins 1992). Traditional methods and examples of pressure garments include compression wraps and self-adhesive elastic tape (Co-Wrap® and Coban®); tubular support bandages (Jobst®, Bio-Concepts®, and Tubigrip®); commercial products (Isotoner® and Jobst Interim Care garments); and custom-fitted garments (Jobst and Bio-Concepts).

Occupational therapists are often responsible for the measurement, ordering, and fitting of pressure garments. Pre-sized garments are usually made in adult sizes, but a limited selection is available for children. Custom pressure garments should be ordered as soon as there is good, dry skin coverage and the patient's weight is stable. Garments must provide an average of 25 mm Hg of tension pressure (Miles and Grigsby 1990) and must be worn continuously and consistently for 23 hours a day for 6 to 18 months to be effective (Binder 1992). When garments are used, two are always ordered to allow washing and air-drying time before reapplication. A water-based lubricating skin cream must be applied regularly, usually twice daily.

When pressure garment fabric must bridge over concave anatomical surfaces, inserts and molds are used to provide conforming pressure. Sterile commercial inserts, such as silastic gel sheeting, are cut and applied directly to the skin. Silicone gel normalizes the texture and color of hypertrophic scarring and reduces the occurrence and subjective complaints of pain and pruritus. Wearing tolerance can be developed over the course of 1 to 2 weeks. The gel and scar must be inspected and cleaned twice daily (Farquhar 1992).

Molds, such as high-density or prosthetic foam and silicone or Silastic® elastomer, require that a catalyst be mixed with a base material before application. Prosthetic foam and silicone elastomer require that the patient be immobilized during setting time. Otoform K™, a Silastic elastomer, has a putty-like consistency and a relatively quick drying time, making it ideal for use with children (Carr-Collins 1992). Bivalve Otoform K or Silastic elastomer circumferential mitts can be designed to provide circumferential pressure and conformity (Malick and Carr 1982).

Scar contractures in interdigital web spaces are common (Leman 1992). Web space inserts are made from thermoplastics, silicone elastomer, or silicone gel and are positioned under custom pressure garments (Leman 1992). Szeliski-Scott (1994) found that self-adhesive tape straps applied directly across the interdigital hand web spaces were the most advantageous due to minimal bulk, optimal contour, ease of application and wear, and cost-effectiveness.

The use of pressure and positioning modalities and circumferential or web space pressure with very young or nonverbal children is difficult due to their miniature body size, rapid growth, interest in active play, perpetual need to inspect new devices, and intolerance of discomfort during measuring and fitting. Fabricating splints during play or while the infant is asleep or sedated may be necessary. Creative strapping solutions may be required to minimize slippage and prevent removal. Frequent remolding, especially in the first 6 months, is required to accommodate for changing contours and growth. Contractures in children are difficult to correct nonsurgically, indicating the importance of early prophylactic splinting. The need for corrective surgery should be avoided but can be expected in the very small, severely burned hand. Heterotopic ossification is a rare complication in pediatric burn patients, but therapists should be familiar with its symptomatology (Koch et al. 1992).

Promoting participation in self-care and play pursuits ensures that patients partake in activities that encourage strengthening, joint mobility, and psychological adjustment. Play is essential to development and central to coping and adapting successfully to trauma and disability (Mahaney 1990). Technical aids are often required to ensure full participation in activities of daily living. The rehabilitation team members aid the patient in dealing with his or her reaction to disfigurement and hospitalization.

Jan Meets Rozmin

On Jan's first day of work as an occupational therapist at ABC-MC, she was introduced to her first client. Rozmin was 16 months old on admission to the burn unit and 18 months old by the time Jan became her primary therapist. Rozmin's medical and social history indicated that she is asthmatic and has had frequent short hospital admissions; she is African-American and has a 13-year-old sister, Rena, and a 5-year-old brother, Martin. Her mother has been a single parent for 10 years. The family receives social assistance and lives in a small two-bedroom apartment 3 miles from ABC-MC. The children are close to their maternal grandmother, who visits Rozmin on a regular basis. Rozmin's mother and siblings visit weekly.

The grandmother indicates that Rozmin is right-handed and that her development has always been age appropriate. She reports that Rozmin's nutritional level prior to this hospitalization was adequate, although Rozmin prefers junk food. The social worker has been unable to determine the name or location of Rozmin's father.

The hospital admission note indicates that Rena was giving Rozmin a bath when Martin inadvertently turned off the cold water tap. Rozmin was immersed in scalding water for approximately 2 minutes before her sister realized what had happened. Although Rena poured cold water on Rozmin's reddened skin, she did not call the ambulance until a few hours later when Rozmin's skin discoloration did not subside. Rozmin's mother was not home at the time.

Rozmin was diagnosed with the most common type of burn among children age 1 to 2—hot water scalds (Binder 1992). She received burns to 40%–50% TBSA, including her lower trunk, buttocks, perineum, both lower legs and feet, and both arms and hands (right > left). On day 7 of her admission, Rozmin received sheet grafts from her back to the dorsum of her left hand and fingers; dorsum of both feet; instep and medial border of her left foot; and lateral border of her right foot.

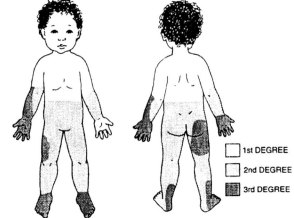

Figure 4.1 Rozmin with Burns—1st, 2nd, and 3rd degree

62

On day 17, Rozmin received a 3:1 meshed graft to her right thigh and buttocks from her back. She had gone septic once, causing this graft to heal poorly. Rozmin's discharge from the hospital had been delayed due to her current nutritional needs, regular rehabilitation service requirements, and her parent's reluctance to manage her burn care. She required light dressings on her right thigh graft site and both feet. Hypertrophic scarring was evident on the dorsum of both hands, both feet, left posterior thigh, and left thigh.

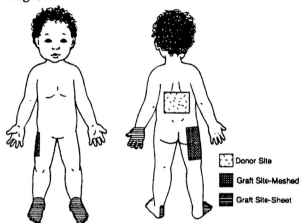

Figure 4.2 Rozmin with Donor-Graft Site—Meshed/Sheet

During Jan's initial treatment session, she notices that Rozmin has lost a few degrees of right elbow extension. Bilateral wrist flexion and extension also are limited. Rozmin's right hand is beginning to show a typical claw hand deformity, due to dorsal skin tightness. At rest, her metacarpal phalangeal (MCP) joints are slightly hyperextended with interphalangeal (IP) joint flexion. Passive range of motion (ROM) is better than active. Rozmin's little finger (5th digit) is becoming tight with MCP extension, IP flexion, and ulnar deviation. Her right thumb opposition and IP flexion are limited.

Rozmin tends to keep her right knee slightly flexed and walks on the lateral border of her left foot. Her buttock skin is tight, and she prefers a reclined position and dislikes the long-leg sit position.

Jan reviewed the ROM assessment from last week; the table follows:

Table 4.1 Range of Motion (ROM) Assessment

Left		Range of Motion		Right	
Passive	Active			Passive	Active
		Shoulder			
180	180	Flexion	0°–180°	180	180
60	60	Extension	0°–60°	60	60
170	170	Abduction	0°–170°	170	170
		Elbow			
150	150	Flexion-Extension	0°–150°	150	130
80	80	Supination	0°–80°	80	80
80	80	Pronation	0°–80°	60	60

continued

Table 4.1 Range of Motion (ROM) Assessment (continued)

Left		Range of Motion		Right	
Passive	Active			Passive	Active
		Wrist			
35	20	Flexion	0°–80°	10	0
60	55	Extension	0°–70°	50	45
25	25	Ulnar Deviation	0°–30°	25	25
20	10	Radial Deviation	0°–20°	10	0
		Index Finger (Digit 2)			
90	90	MP Flexion	0°–90°	60	40
45	45	MP Hyperextension	0°–45°	30	20
100	100	PIP Extension-Flexion	0°–100°	0–90	0–60
90	90	DIP Flexion	0°–90°	70	60
15	15	DIP Hyperextension	0°–15°	10	0
Full	Full	Abduction		Full	¾ range
Full	Full	Adduction		Full	Not full (swelling)
		Middle Finger (Digit 3)			
90	90	MP Flexion	0°–90°	60	45
45	45	MP Hyperextension	0°–45°	20	10
100	100	PIP Extension-Flexion	0°–100°	0–90	0–60
90	90	DIP Flexion	0°–90°	70	60
15	15	DIP Hyperextension	0°–15°	10	10
Full	Full	Abduction		Full	Unassessable
Full	Full	Adduction		Full	Not full
		Ring Finger (Digit 4)			
90	90	MP Flexion	0°–90°	50	40
45	45	MP Hyperextension	0°–45°	30	15
100	100	PIP Extension-Flexion	0°–100°	0–80	0–60
90	90	DIP Flexion	0°–90°	70	60
15	15	DIP Hyperextension	0°–15°	0	0
Full	Full	Abduction		Full	½ range
Full	Full	Adduction		Full	Full
		Little Finger (Digit 5)			
75	50	MP Flexion	0°–90°	50	20
30	20	MP Extension	0°–45°	25	10
50	45	PIP Extension-Flexion	0°–100°	45	0–30
0–90	0–90	DIP Flexion	0°–90°	0–70	60
0	0	DIP Hyperextension	0°–15°	0	0
Ulnar deviation	Ulnar deviation	Abduction		10° Ulnar deviation	Minimal mobility
Neutral	Neutral	Adduction		Neutral	
		Thumb			
15	15	CM Flexion	0°–15°	15	15
20	20	CM Extension	0°–20°	15	neutral
50	50	MP Extension-Flexion	0°–50°	0–45	0–45
80	80	IP Flexion	0°–80°	0–60	45
10	10	IP Hyperextension	10°	0	10
70	70	Abduction	0°–70°	70	50
Full	Full	Opposition	cm	Full	Large objects only

continued

Table 4.1 Range of Motion (ROM) Assessment (continued)

Left		Range of Motion		Right	
Passive	Active			Passive	Active
		Hip			
120	110	Flexion	0°–120°	100	90
20	20	Extension	0°–30°	20	20
45	45	Abduction	0°–45°	45	45
30	20	Adduction	0°–30°	20	20
25	10	Internal Rotation	0°–45°	25	10
45	45	External Rotation	0°–45°	45	45
		Knee			
0–135	0–135	Extension-Flexion	0°–135°	0–125	15–125
		Ankle			
20	20	Dorsiflexion	0°–20°	20	20
50	50	Plantar flexion	0°–50°	50	50
35	35	Inversion	0°–35°	10	0
10	0	Eversion	0°–20°	20	20

Rozmin wore her bilateral foot drop splints throughout the night and her right hand antideformity splint at night and nap time. See Figure 4.3.

Figure 4.3 Antideformity Splint

After her second grafting surgery procedure, Rozmin's hands were casted while she was under anesthetic for a dressing change. The mold was sent to the manufacturer to ensure custom fit. These hand garments were made with a zipper and open fingertips to improve fit and sensation.

A few days after Jan starts seeing Rozmin, the custom pressure hand and sock garments arrive. Unfortunately, Jan is unable to get these garments on Rozmin. The finger sections are too small. Rozmin has either grown or her skin condition has changed too much. Jan can order another set or simply try other pressure alternatives for now.

Rozmin's custom socks fit. Jan will have to measure and order pants and a right-sleeve pressure garment. For about 2 weeks, Rozmin has been wearing elastic tubing (Tubigrip®) on her legs and right arm and has an adhesive bandage wrap (Coban®) on her hands. The nurses, Rozmin's grandmother, and sister wash Rozmin's Tubigrip® garments regularly.

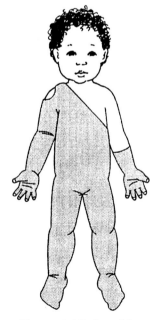

Figure 4.4 Baby with Garments—Optimal Fit

Jan often takes Rozmin to the playroom at ABC-MC where Rozmin enjoys watching children play with pop-up toys, a small toy piano, and soap-blow bubbles. She is, however, difficult to engage in play and appears happiest when she sees her grandmother.

Jan is informed that Rozmin will be discharged in 10 to 14 days, so she sets up an appointment to spend some time with the physical therapist. Burn team rounds are scheduled for Friday, and Jan needs to participate in discharge planning. A family conference has been scheduled to begin next week. Although all parents are invited to monthly burn-care presentations, Rozmin's mother has not attended. The nursing staff, however, has involved the family in garment care and cleaning. ABC-MC burn unit library has literature and videotapes for families.

Jan needs to identify the role of occupational therapy in discharge preparation and to prioritize her intervention objectives. Rozmin's hands need attention.

The Challenge

Assume that Jan's challenges and responsibilities are your own. Use the information that you have been provided to determine your role as Rozmin's therapist. What are the discharge priorities, and how will you spend the next 10 to 14 days? If you would like assistance, use the questions and following resources to aid your analysis. Complete questions 1, 2, 5-8 at a minimum.

Questions to Aid Analysis

1. What are the skills and abilities of an 18-month-old child? Can you classify these abilities into occupational performance areas and performance components using *Uniform Terminology* (American Occupational Therapy Association 1994)?

2. Describe the developmental stage of early childhood according to Erik Erikson, Arnold Gesell, Jean Piaget, and Robert Havighurst. What do these theorists tell you about Rozmin's sensorimotor, cognitive, communication, social-emotional, and self-help skill development and needs?

3. Describe the role and function of occupational therapy in burn care. In what phase of treatment is Rozmin?

4. Describe the quality of burned skin and hypertrophic scarring at Rozmin's stage of recovery. How do the physiological characteristics of hypertrophic scars influence the care and treatment of Rozmin's injury?

5. Given what you have learned about burn care and treatment and the developmental abilities and needs of an 18-month-old child, what are your goals as Rozmin's therapist? Ensure that your goals maintain or promote function, prevent dysfunction, and fit the concerns, priorities, and resources of this family. Be prepared to modify these goals after meeting with the team and with Rozmin's family.

    Goal 1:

    Goal 2:

    Goal 3:

    Goal 4:

    Goal 5:

6. To address your joint integrity goals, determine which joints have lost ROM or require prophylactic treatment to maintain full range. In what position would you like each of these joints to be placed? What are your options to maintain or gain joint range of motion? What will you recommend as a wearing and cleaning schedule? How will you know when these orthotics need to be changed or terminated?

7. To address your scar management goals, determine which skin areas require conforming pressure. How will you achieve conforming pressure? Which method will you use to manage the hypertropic scarring on Rozmin's hands? How will you measure and order Rozmin's lower extremity and right arm garments? Why do you think this traditional garment measurement process was not appropriate for Rozmin's hands? Will you order any special options (e.g., zippers) to simplify garment management and enhance compliance?

    Assume that you would like to use Coban® wrap or self-adhesive tape to maintain Rozmin's hand web spaces. How would you wrap this material? Would you let other staff apply this modality? What type of training and risk would be involved in this treatment strategy?

    Assume that you would like to use thin foam straps attached to a wristband for maintaining web spaces, a volar antideformity splint, and a pressure garment. What would your recommended wearing schedule be? Could any of these strategies be used simultaneously?

    Hypertrophic scarring is beginning in Rozmin's groin and buttock region. She is not toilet trained and wears diapers. How would you handle this situation? When will you discontinue pressure treatment? What are the characteristics of a mature scar?

8. What are some of the complications from pressure or splint application that you and Rozmin's caregivers must monitor?

9. What are the funding sources for inpatient and outpatient splints and pressure garments?

10. Use your creative play talents to develop some passive and active ROM and muscle strengthening treatment activities and to elicit cooperation from Rozmin. Ensure that your recommendations are meaningful and purposeful. The more functional the activity, the more likely others will be able to carry out the activities.

11. Describe your plans for family training (who, what, how).

12. Attitudes and beliefs shape and determine behaviors and our relationships with others. Do you have any personal values that may influence your interaction with Rozmin's mother? Describe your values and determine if they reflect the core values and attitudes of occupational therapy practice (American Occupational Therapy Association 1993). Plan your session with this family to ensure that you establish rapport and a healthy relationship.

13. Multidisciplinary teams collaborate to coordinate care. Which topics will you need to discuss with the physician, dietitian, nurse, physical therapist, social worker, and psychologist? How will you ensure that this communication occurs?

14. What will be the role of the outpatient or home health therapist?

New Terminology

3:1 meshed grafts	heterotopic ossification	septic shock
antideformity splints	hypertrophic scar	serial casting
bivalve	keloid scar	Silastic elastomer
claw hand deformity	partial thickness	silastic gel sheeting
debridement	prosthetic foam	silicone elastomer
elastomer	pruritus	silicone gel
full thickness	ROM	TBSA
grafts		

Learning Resources

Canadian occupational therapists should use the uniform terminology proposed in the Client-Centred Model of Occupational Performance outlined in Appendix C.

Most of the therapeutic materials described in this module are available from the following companies:

Northcoast Medical
187 Stauffer Boulevard
San Jose, CA 95125-1042
1-800-821-9319

Sammons
A Bissell Healthcare Company
P.O. Box 386
Western Springs, IL 60558-0386
1-800-323-5547

Smith and Nephew Rolyan
One Quality Drive, P.O. Box 1005
Germantown, WI 53022
1-800-558-8633

American Occupational Therapy Association. 1993. Core values and attitudes of occupational therapy practice. *American Journal of Occupational Therapy* 47:1085–86.

American Occupational Therapy Association. 1994. Uniform terminology for occupational therapy, 3d ed. *American Journal of Occupational Therapy* 48:1047–54.

Binder, H. 1992. Rehabilitation of the burned child, In *Pediatric Rehabilitation*, 2d ed., edited by G. E. Molnar. Baltimore: Williams & Wilkins.

Carr-Collins, J. A. 1992. Pressure techniques for the prevention of hypertrophic scar. *Clinics in Plastic Surgery* 19:733–43.

Case-Smith, J., A. S. Allen, and P. N. Pratt. 1996. *Occupational therapy for children.* 3d ed. St. Louis: C. V. Mosby.

Chan, S. W., and L. W. Pedretti. 1990. Burns. In *Occupational therapy: Practice skills for physical dysfunction*, 3d ed., edited by L. W. Pedretti and B. Zoltan. St. Louis: C. V. Mosby.

Cosman, B. 1982. The burned child. In *The child with disabling illness: Principles of rehabilitation.* Downey, J. A., and N. L. Low. New York: Raven Press.

Hunter, J., E. J. Mackin, and A. D. Callahan. 1994. *Rehabilitation of the hand: Surgery and therapy*, 4th ed. St. Louis: C. V. Mosby.

Jordan, C., and R. Allely. 1996. Burns and burn rehabilitation. In *Occupational therapy practice skills for physical dysfunction*, 4th ed., edited by L. W. Pedretti. St. Louis: C. V. Mosby.

Malick, M. H., and J. A. Carr. 1982. *Manual on management of the burn patient.* Pittsburgh: Harmarville Rehabilitation Center, Educational Resource Division.

Mercer, N. S. G. 1984. Silicone gel in the treatment of keloid scars. *British Journal of Plastic Surgery* 83–87.

Schwanholt, C., M. B. Dautherty, T. Gaboury, and G. D. Warden. 1992. Splinting the pediatric palmar burn. *Journal of Burn Care and Rehabilitation* 13:460–64.

Sullivan, T., J. Smith, J. Kermode, E. McIver, and D. J. Courtemanche. 1990. Rating the burn scar. *Journal of Burn Care and Rehabilitation* 11:256–60.

Ward, R. S., R. Reddy, C. Brockway, C. Hayes-Lundy, and P. Mills. 1994. Use of Coban® self-adhesive wrap in management of post hand grafts: Case reports. *Journal of Burn Care and Rehabilitation* 15:364–69.

Focus on Research

Children in infancy typically receive scald burns, whereas toddlers are injured by scald and contact thermal burns. School-age children typically suffer flame burns and adolescents sustain electrical burns. Two percent of all burns occur in children less than one year old, 20% occur in children 5 years old or younger, and 36% occur in children 10 years old or younger (Lynch 1979).

Loss of joint motion in a child's hand causes a more significant loss of function than in an adult hand. The most common upper extremity burn deformities include

- claw hand deformity with ulnar deviation and ulnar rotation,
- flattening of the longitudinal and transverse arches,
- boutonniere deformity in dorsal burns, and
- delayed flexion contracture of the fifth digit

(Carr-Collins 1992; Leman 1992).

Abuse-related scald burn victims are more likely than non-abused scalded children to be part of a broken home; have a single, unemployed parent; and have a young mother (Hummel et al. 1993). Victims tend to be the younger or youngest child in a larger-than-expected and economically disadvantaged family (Libber and Stayton 1984). Compliance with burn rehabilitation follow-up in abuse cases is poor.

Compliance with treatment regimes after discharge is important as burn care will require long-term garment use and frequent refitting. Burn scars may not keep up with eventual bone growth or breast development. Sunlight must be avoided as hypertrophic tissue is prone to sunburn and hyperpigmentation, and garments are completely inadequate for sun protection. Literature indicates that parental and peer support are major contributors to higher levels of self-esteem and adaptation in burned children (Doctor 1992).

References

American Burn Association. *Aims of the American Burn Association: Preventing, care, teaching, research*. New Orleans: American Burn Association.

Binder, H. 1992. Rehabilitation of the burned child. In *Pediatric Rehabilitation*, 2d ed., edited by D. E. Molnar. Baltimore: Williams & Wilkins.

Carr-Collins, J. A. 1992. Pressure treatment for the prevention of hypertrophic scar. *Clinics in Plastic Surgery* 19:733–43.

Carvajal, H. F. 1990. Burns in children and adolescents: Initial management as the first step in successful rehabilitation. *Pediatrician* 17:237–43.

Deitch, E. A., T. M. Wheelahan, M. P. Rose, J. Clothier and J. Cotter. 1983. Hypertrophic burn scars: Analysis of variables. *Journal of Trauma* 23:895–98.

Doctor, M. E. 1992. Helping the burned child to adapt. *Clinics in Plastic Surgery* 19:607-14.

Farquhar, K. 1992. Silicone gel and hypertrophic scar formation: A literature review. *Canadian Journal of Occupational Therapy* 59:78–86.

Hummel, R. P., D. G. Greenhalgh, P. P. Barthel, C. M. DeSerna, M. M. Gottschlich, L. E. James, and G. D. Warden. 1993. Outcome and socioeconomic aspects of suspected child abuse scald burns. *Journal of Burn Care and Rehabilitation* 14:121-26.

Koch, B. M., C. M. Wu, J. Randolph, and G. D. Eng. 1992. Heterotopic ossification in children with burns: Two case reports. *Archives of Physical Medicine and Rehabilitation* 73:1104–06.

Leman, C. J. 1992. Splints and accessories following burn reconstruction. *Clinics in Plastic Surgery* 19:721–31.

Libber, S. M., and D. J. Stayton. 1984. Childhood burns reconsidered: The child, the family, the burn injury. *Journal of Trauma* 24:245.

Lynch, J. B. 1979. Thermal burns. In *Plastic Surgery*, 3d ed., edited by W. C. Grabb and J. W. Smith. Boston: Little, Brown.

Mahaney, N. B. 1990. Restoration of play in a severely burned three-year-old child. *Journal of Burn Care and Rehabilitation* 11:57–63.

Malick, M. H., and J. A. Carr. 1982. *Manual on management of the burn patient.* Pittsburgh: Harmarville Rehabilitation Center, Educational Resource Division.

Miles, W., and L. Grigsby. 1990. Remodeling of scar tissue in the burned hand. In *Rehabilitation of the hand: Surgery and therapy*, 3d ed., edited by J. M. Hunter, L. H. Schneider, E. J. Mackin, and A. D. Callahan, 841–57. St. Louis: C. V. Mosby.

Ridgeway, C. L., M. B. Daugherty, and G. D. Warden. 1991. Serial casting as a technique to correct burn scar contractures: A case report. *Journal of Burn Care Rehabilitation* 12:67–72.

Salisbury, R. E., S. U. Reeves, and P. Wright. 1990. Acute care and rehabilitation of the burned hand. In *Rehabilitation of the hand: Surgery and therapy*, edited by J. M. Hunter, L. H. Schneider, E. J. Mackin, and A. D. Callahan, 831–40. St. Louis: C. V. Mosby.

Szeliski-Scott, B. 1994. *New Techniques to preserve web spaces in burns.* Poster presentation, Canadian and American Occupational Therapy Conference, Boston.

Simon (Part 1)

Background

Simon is a 3-year 6-month-old child who lives with his parents and younger sister on Ancestor Reservation. The family owns a small home without running water or electricity. Simon's grandparents live on the same property in a separate house. His mother works part-time as a child-care worker; his father is a reservation police officer; and his grandfather is a local elder. Simon attends a day-care center three days per week when his mother works.

ABC Family Services (ABC-FS) provides multidisciplinary, family-centered evaluation and intervention to infants and toddlers with disabilities within day-care and home settings. ABC-FS employs one nurse, Sonya, and one part-time physical therapist, James.

During one visit to the day-care center, Sonya noticed that Simon had great difficulty following directions and that he watched his sister for visual cues. He had difficulty following verbal directions and did not talk much. The day-care workers described him as clumsy. His parents were concerned that he had difficulty articulating words in English and in their traditional language.

Lori Meets Simon

Lori has just been hired as the team's first occupational therapist. During her first week of work, Lori initiates a home screening at Sonya's request. As a new visitor, Lori finds the family's interpersonal style particularly challenging. Simon's parents appear shy and hesitant. They do not establish or maintain eye contact with Lori. A relationship is not developed during this first meeting.

Lori: *(Speaking to Simon's mother)* Would you agree that Simon has difficulty saying his words and is kind of clumsy?

Mother: *(With her head lowered, answers quietly)* Yes, but Simon's family understands him.

Lori: Would you like me to assist Simon's day-care workers with understanding him?

Mother: Yes, that would be good.

Lori: Would you like me to work with Simon to help him be less clumsy?

Simon's mother shrugs her shoulders. She does not seem concerned about this area or its significance. Her priority is speech development.

FirstSTEp™
Screening Test for Evaluating Preschoolers

Record Form

Child's Name Simon Gender m

School

Teacher

Examiner Lori

Age Groups 1&2

	Year	Month	Day
Date Tested			
Date of Birth			
Age	3	6	

Age Group	Age Range
1 =	2:9—3:2
2 =	3.3—3.8

Age Group 1

Domain Score	Cognitive (Raw Score)	Language (Raw Score)	Motor (Raw Score)	Social-Emotional (Raw Score)	Adaptive Behavior (Raw Score)	Parent/Teacher (Raw Score)	Domain Score
19	—	20-23	—	—	64-72	—	19
18	17	19	—	—	59-63	—	18
17	16	18	15	—	55-58	—	17
16	15	17	14	—	51-54	—	16
15	14	16	13	—	47-50	—	15
14	13	15	12	66	43-46	40	14
13	12	14	11	65	39-42	—	13
12	11	12-13	10	64	35-38	39	12
11	10	11	9	62-63	31-34	38	11
10	9	10	8	60-61	27-30	37	10
9	8	9	7	58-59	21-26	35-36	9
8	7	8	6	56-57	15-20	33-34	8
7	6	7	5	52-55	11-14	31-32	7
6	5	6	4	49-51	8-10	29-30	6
5	4	5	3	44-48	6-7	26-28	5
4	3	4	2	40-43	4-5	23-25	4
3	2	3	1	36-39	2-3	20-22	3
2	1	2	0	32-35	0-1	17-19	2
1	0	0-1	—	0-31	—	0-16	1

Domain Scores ( ) + ( ) + ( ) [ ] [ ] [ ]

Sum of Domain Scores ( ) = Composite Score ( )

Age Group 2

Domain Score	Cognitive (Raw Score)	Language (Raw Score)	Motor (Raw Score)	Social-Emotional (Raw Score)	Adaptive Behavior (Raw Score)	Parent/Teacher (Raw Score)	Domain Score
19	—	22-23	—	—	—	—	19
18	—	21	—	—	72	—	18
17	—	20	—	—	68-71	—	17
16	17	19	15	—	64-67	—	16
15	16	18	14	—	60-63	—	15
14	15	17	13	66	56-59	40	14
13	14	16	—	—	51-55	—	13
12	13	14-15	12	65	45-50	39	12
11	12	13	—	64	39-44	38	11
10	11	12	11	62-63	33-38	37	10
9	10	11	10	60-61	27-32	35-36	9
8	9	10	9	58-59	21-26	33-34	8
7	8	9	8	56-57	15-20	31-32	7
6	7	8	7	52-55	11-14	29-30	6
5	6	7	6	48-51	8-10	26-28	5
4	5	6	5	44-47	6-7	23-25	4
3	4	5	4	40-43	4-5	20-22	3
2	3	4	3	36-39	2-3	17-19	2
1	0-2	0-3	0-2	0-35	0-1	0-16	1

Domain Scores ( ) + ( ) + ( ) [ ] [ ] [ ]

Sum of Domain Scores ( ) = Composite Score ( )

SUM OF DOMAIN SCORES

SUM OF DOMAIN SCORES	3	4	5	6	7	8	9	10	11	12	13	14	15	16	17	18	19	20	21	22	23	24	25	26	27	28	29	30
COMPOSITE SCORES	13	14	16	17	18	19	21	22	23	25	26	27	29	30	31	33	34	35	37	38	40	41	43	44	45	47	48	49

SUM OF DOMAIN SCORES	31	32	33	34	35	36	37	38	39	40	41	42	43	44	45	46	47	48	49	50	51	52	53	54	55	56	57
COMPOSITE SCORES	50	51	52	53	55	57	58	60	61	63	65	67	69	71	73	75	77	79	81	83	85	87	89	91	93	95	97

Figure 4.5 *FirstSTEP* Record Form

Indicates scores in the Green range

Indicates scores in the Yellow range

Indicates scores in the Red range

Adaptive Behavior Checklist

Ratings Key:
0 = Rarely or never independently   1 = Sometimes independently, usually with assistance   2 = Usually or always independently

Age Groups 1 & 2

Daily Living

Dressing
Dresses for bed — (0) 1 2
Correctly distinguishes front from back of clothes — 0 1 (2)
Tells if right side is out — 0 (1) 2
Puts heel of sock in correct place — (0) 1 2
Dresses completely except for some fasteners — (0) 1 2

Feeding
Holds spoon with thumb and 2nd and 3rd fingers — 0 (1) 2
Eats most food with no spilling; uses spoon or fork — (0) 1 2

Grooming
Brushes teeth if toothbrush made ready — (0) 1 2
Blows nose when requested — 0 (1) 2
Has daytime toileting control with occasional accidents — 0 (1) 2
Dries self with towel except back — 0 (1) 2
Handles comb well; combs but does not part hair — (0) 1 2

Self-Management and Social Interaction

Independence
Understands concept of last year/next year — 0 (1) 2
Understands concept of day before yesterday/day after tomorrow — 0 (1) 2
Chooses clothing specific to weather conditions — 0 1 (2)

Self-Managed Play
Plays independently for 1 hour (e.g., on playground) — (0) 1 2
Initiates dramatic play with complex theme, not just roles — (0) 1 2
Differentiates between real and make-believe (e.g., a real plate but pretend food) — 0 (1) 2

Personal Responsibility
Chooses when to break rules; has a reason for doing so — 0 1 (2)

Interactions with Others
Sits and converses with adult through a 30-minute meal — (0) 1 2
Participates in simple interactive games (e.g., playing "house") — (0) 1 2
Waits 2–5 minutes for a turn in group activity — 0 (1) 2
Cooperates in play with another child; shares toys and understands common themes — 0 (1) 2
Plays complex interactive games (e.g., tag, hide and seek) with children — 0 (1) 2
Chooses fairly regular group of friends to play with — 0 (1) 2

Functioning Within the Community

Mobility
Runs well and turns abruptly while running — 0 (1) 2
Catches small ball from 3 feet — (0) (1) 2
Colors mostly inside the lines — (0) 1 2

Communication
Relates his/her daily life experiences — 0 (1) 2
Relates experiences of other family members — (0) 1 2
Relates fanciful tales, fairy tales, jokes, or TV show plots — (0) 1 2
Remembers two directions (e.g., put the ball there and the hat here) — (0) 1 2

Social Adaptation
Knows which way to turn to go from home to familiar place — 0 (1) 2
Knows function of helpers (e.g., fire fighter, doctor, police officer) — 0 (1) 2
Knows landmarks outside of immediate neighborhood (e.g., airport, river, big tower) — 0 (1) 2

Social Responsibility
Correctly identifies emotions in others (e.g., happy, sad, angry) — 0 (1) 2

Raw Score [25] **Total**

Figure 4.6 *FirstSTEP* Adaptive Behavior Checklist—Age Groups 1 & 2

Lori completes the FirstSTEP Screening Test for Evaluating Preschoolers *(Miller 1993) during her visit with this family. She administers this test in English. Simon's parents quietly observe the session and appear pleased that Simon enjoys the activities. See Figures 4.5 and 4.6.*

Lori leaves the family's home questioning the purpose of the visit. Who wants help for this child? What are the family's priorities? Would intervention become a priority to the family? After talking with Sonya and James, Lori discovers that some families view intervention with caution. Establishing rapport will take time, and Lori will benefit from patiently allowing the relationship to grow as she demonstrates the resources she can provide. An important part of this culture is to be polite and to listen without interrupting. Lori's team reassures her that she will learn and eventually understand the best way to provide services to Simon's family.

The Challenge

You are Lori. What are your impressions of Simon? What do you recommend as an occupational therapist? If you would like assistance with this challenge, use the following questions and resources to aid your analysis. See Selected Answers in Appendix E.

Questions to Aid Analysis

1. What are the activities, tasks, and roles of a 3-year 6-month-old child. What skills and abilities do you expect Simon to possess? Describe the developmental stage of early childhood according to Eric Erikson, Arnold Gesell, Jean Piaget, and Robert Havighurst. What do these theorists tell you about Simon's sensorimotor, cognitive, communication, social-emotional, and self-help skill development and needs?

2. How will you identify Simon's parents' goals and objectives? How will you describe the service and resources occupational therapy has to offer?

3. Is the *FirstSTEP* the best choice of a screening test to use with this child? Should special considerations be made when interpreting *FirstSTEP* scores with a minority child (Miller 1993, 100–102)?

4. What does Simon's performance on the *FirstSTEP* suggest about his strengths and limitations and the need for further evaluation? (See Simon's scores in Appendix D.) How does this information assist with your interpretation of Simon's performance? Determine Simon's percentile rank equivalent for the domain and composite scores (Miller 1993, Table 4.13, 109).

   How does the *FirstSTEP* color-coded classification (green, yellow, and red—top to bottom) assist you in interpreting Simon's performance to his parents? Classifications are shown as shades of gray in Figure 4.5.

Using the *FirstSTEP* in this context will enable you to become familiar with its use and potential. Prior to actual test administration, users should study the manual and use the Procedural Reliability Checklist (Miller 1993, 136-37) to ensure competency of administration and interpretation.

5. What do you think about the Parent/Teacher Scale domain score?

6. What further information do you need to complete this screening? Do you have all of the information required to determine whether a complete evaluation is appropriate? What are your recommendations as an occupational therapist? Write your screening report.

New Terminology

family-centered
FirstSTEP
mean
screening
standard deviation

Learning Resources

Case-Smith, J. 1993. *Pediatric occupational therapy and early intervention*. Stoneham, MA: Andover Medical Publishers.

Clark, S., and S. D. Kelley. 1992. Traditional Native American values: Conflict or concordance in rehabilitation? *Journal of Rehabilitation* 58:23–28.

Lynch, E. W., and M. J. Hanson. 1992. *Developing cross-cultural competence: A guide for working with young children and their families*. Baltimore: Paul H. Brookes.

Meadows, J. L. 1991. Multicultural communication. *Physical and Occupational Therapy in Pediatrics* 11:31–42.

Miller, L. J. 1993. *FirstSTEP: Screening test for evaluating preschoolers*. San Antonio, TX: The Psychological Corporation. (See Appendix A.)

Reference

Miller, L. J. 1993. *FirstSTEP: Screening test for evaluating preschoolers*. San Antonio, TX: The Psychological Corporation.

Simon (Part 2)

It has been two weeks since Lori first met Simon and his family. She has just completed collecting information for her initial evaluation and will begin the process of program planning.

Lori believes that Simon's performance on the *FirstSTEP* indicates the need for a comprehensive evaluation. She selects the *Miller Assessment for Preschoolers* (MAP) (Miller 1988) for this purpose. After completing this assessment, Lori begins to give some thought to the type of program she will recommend for Simon and his family. (See Figure 4.7.) The names used in Figure 4.7 are hypothetical.

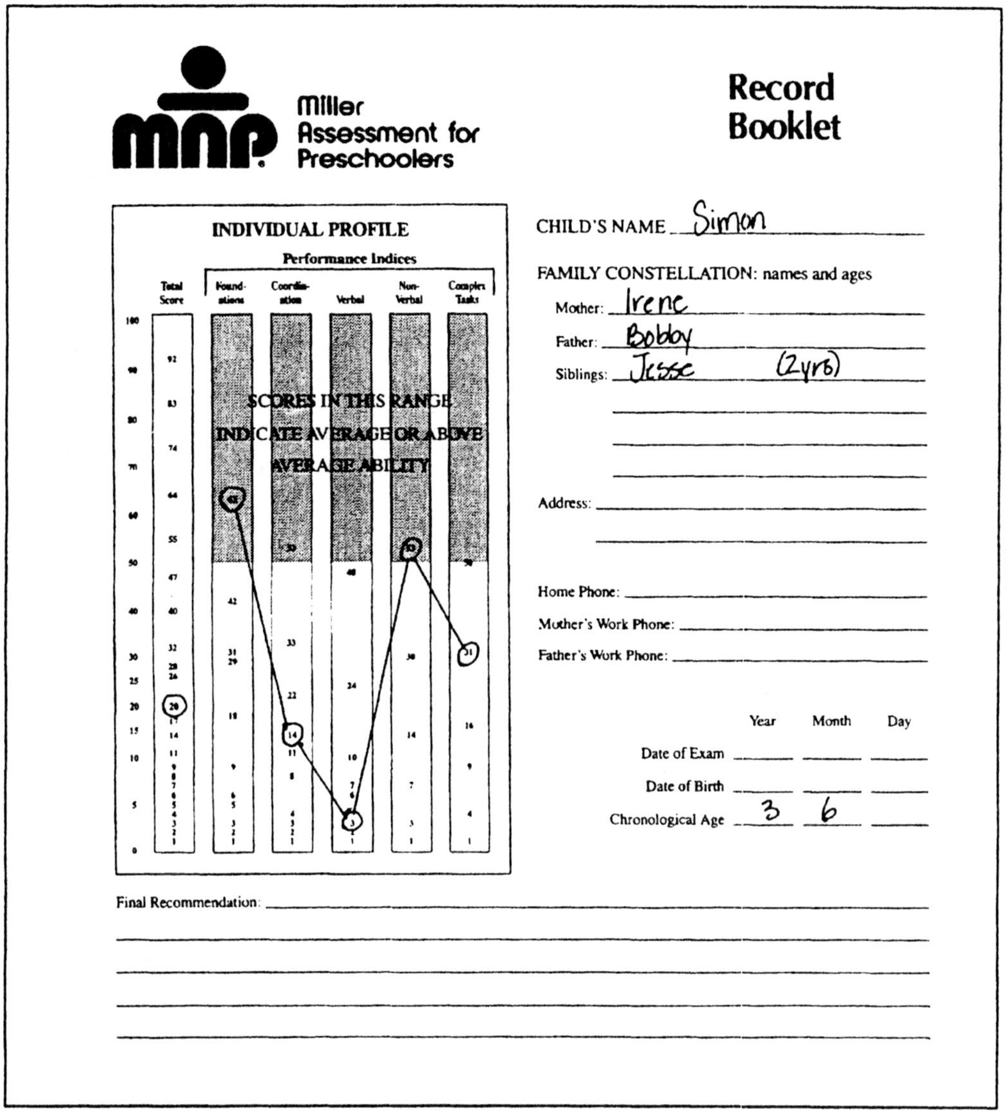

Figure 4.7 MAP Record Form for Simon

The Challenge

You are Lori. What are your impressions regarding Simon's performance on the MAP (Miller 1998). What are your recommendations regarding the provision of occupational therapy services? Will you seek assistance or make referrals to other health professionals? If you would like assistance with this challenge, use the questions and resources below to aid your analysis.

Questions to Aid Analysis

1. Is the MAP (Miller 1998) the best choice of assessment to use with this child? When interpreting the MAP scores for minority children, what special considerations should be made? How will you determine whether the test content is socioculturally applicable and valid? Explain your reasoning.

2. What does Simon's performance on the MAP (Miller 1988) suggest about his strengths and limitations? See Figure 4.7.

    How does the MAP (Miller 1988) assist you with determining Simon's risk profile?

    Using the MAP (Miller 1988) in this context will enable you to become familiar with its use and potential. Formal training, practice apprenticeships, and qualified peer reviews are required for competency in test administration and interpretation.

3. What is your impression of the impact of Simon's skills and abilities, as measured by the performance indices of the MAP (Miller 1988), and on his adaptive behaviors, as measured by the Adaptive Behavior Checklist of the *FirstSTEP* (Miller 1993). How do these skills, abilities, and behaviors impact Simon's success as son, brother, and day-care student?

4. What more do you know about this child after completing the MAP (Miller 1988)? What are your recommendations regarding Simon's need for occupational therapy services? Will you seek assistance or make referrals to other health professionals? If you are unable to access any other professional services, what would you do?

5. What are family-centered services and how will they influence your practice as a therapist? Many North American indigenous cultures value community and extended families. How could you include these individuals in the therapeutic process? Could you let the community design a program with your guidance?

6. How will you develop an understanding of Simon's home, family, and community to ensure that your approach is culturally sensitive? What resources can you use in the development of a family-centered, culturally sensitive program plan?

7. "All birds, even those of the same species, are not alike, and it is the same with animals and with human beings. The reason Wakantanka does not make two birds, or animals, or human beings exactly alike is because each is placed here by Wakantanka to be an independent individual and to rely upon itself."* (Shooter, late 19th century, Teton Sioux). Does this quotation influence your perceptions of this child and his family?

8. "The American Indian is of the soil, whether it be the region of the forests, plains, pueblos, or mesas. He fits into the landscape, for the hand that fashioned the continent also fashioned the man for his surrounding"* (Luther Standing Bear [1868?-1939] Oglala Sioux chief). Therapeutic approaches in native communities must be holistic. The mind, body, emotions, and spirit must all work together for a person to be healthy. How could you use this wisdom to teach and learn together with this family and community?

New Terminology

family-centered
MAP

Learning Resources

Information on the MAP (Miller 1988) is provided in Appendix A.

Case-Smith, J. 1993. *Pediatric occupational therapy and early intervention.* Stoneham, MA: Andover Medical Publishers.

Clark, S., and S. D. Kelley. 1992. Traditional Native American values: Conflict or concordance in rehabilitation? *Journal of Rehabilitation* 58:23-28.

Daniels, L. 1990. The *Miller assessment for preschoolers:* Analysis of score patterns for children with developmental delays. *Canadian Journal of Occupational Therapy* 57:205-10.

Deloria, V. 1985. *American Indian policy in the twentieth century.* Norman, OK: University of Oklahoma Press.

DeMars, P. A. 1992. An occupational therapy life skills curriculum model for a Native American tribe: A health promotion program based on ethnographic field research. *American Journal of Occupational Therapy* 46:727-36.

Gilland, H., and J. Rayhner. 1988. *Teaching the Native Americans.* Dubuque, IA: Kendall, Hunt.

---

*From *Native American Wisdom.* 1993. Philadelphia: Running Press. Reprinted with permission.

Johnson, D., E. Paisano, and M. J. Revin. U.S. Department of Commerce and Bureau of Census. 1982. *We: The first Americans.* Washington, D.C.: U.S. Government Printing Press.

Lynch, E. W., and M. J. Hanson. 1992. *Developing cross-cultural competence: A guide for working with young children and their families.* Baltimore: Paul H. Brookes.

Meadows, J. L. 1991. Multicultural communication. *Physical and Occupational Therapy in Pediatrics* 11:31–42.

Miller, L. J. 1988. *Miller assessment for preschoolers: Administration and interpretation seminar handbook.* San Antonio, TX: The Psychological Corporation.

Miller, L. J. 1988. *Miller assessment for preschoolers: Manual–revised.* San Antonio, TX: The Psychological Corporation.

Miller, L. J. 1993. *FirstSTEP: Screening test for evaluating preschoolers.* San Antonio, TX: The Psychological Corporation.

Olson, J. S., and R. Wilson. 1984. *Native Americans in the twentieth century.* Champaign, IL: University of Illinois Press.

Rhoades, E. R., J. Hammond, T. K. Welty, A. O. Handler, and R. W. Amler. 1987. The Indian burden of illness and future health interventions. *Public Health Reports* July-August, 102:361–68.

Schaaf, R. C., and L. L. Mulrooney. 1989. Occupational therapy in early intervention: A family-centered approach. *American Journal of Occupational Therapy* 43:745–54.

Stacey, K. 1994. Contextual assessment of young children: Moving from the strange to the familiar and from theory to praxis. *Child Language Teaching Therapy* 10:179–98.

Reference

Miller, L. J. 1988. *Miller assessment for preschoolers: Manual–Revised.* San Antonio, TX: The Psychological Corporation.

Pierre

Background

ABC Intermediate Unit and Family Service Program provides multidisciplinary evaluation and intervention services to infants and toddlers with developmental disabilities and employs one occupational therapist full-time and four therapists part-time. As the occupational therapy supervisor, Helene has many administrative, managerial, and clinical responsibilities. Current economic pressures within the health-care industry demand that occupational therapists strive for continuous quality improvement (CQI). Helene wants to be a part of that process.

Helene specializes in providing consultation and training to parents, teachers, and caregivers of children with mental retardation. She spends many hours discussing her observations and recommendations with individuals from these groups and writing consultation reports. Helene hopes that these documents

- reinforce occupational therapists' contribution to the multidisciplinary team,
- validate the need to address performance and environmental components to develop, restore, or maintain occupational engagement and prevent dysfunction, and
- promote the development of clinical reasoning, accountability, and quality care.

Three weeks ago, Helene and two other occupational therapists attended a seminar on health and medical documentation. During the drive back to the center, the therapists discussed the historical trend toward standardization of occupational therapy terminology and documentation. The American Occupational Therapy Association (AOTA) first published *Uniform Terminology for Reporting Occupational Therapy Services* in 1979 and the *Guidelines for Occupational Therapy Documentation* seven years later (American Occupational Therapy Association 1986). In 1989 and 1994, the second and third editions of *Uniform Terminology* were published in the *American Journal of Occupational Therapy*. These articles recommended that the occupational therapy record include information on client background, assessment, treatment planning, program implementation, and discontinuation of services.

The Canadian Department of National Health and Welfare (DNHW) and the Canadian Association of Occupational Therapists (CAOT) developed *Guidelines for the Client-Centred Practice of Occupational Therapy* in 1983 (Canadian Department of National Health and Welfare and Canadian Association of Occupational Therapists 1983). These guidelines indicate that evaluation and documentation must include occupational performance area, performance components, and performance context (Canadian Association of Occupational Therapists 1991, 27–28). CAOT's position paper on the role of occupational therapy in pediatrics suggests that a child's occupational performance includes self-care, productivity, and leisure. Performance components include motor, sensory integrative, cognitive, psychological, and social domains (Canadian Association of Occupational Therapists 1991).

Helene wondered whether these categories of concern to the occupational therapist could serve as appropriate headings for occupational therapy reports and discussed the possibility with the other therapists. Helene's colleague, Tina, proposed that occupational therapy reports be formatted to directly reflect the domains of developmental concern to early intervention workers, as described in the Individuals with Disabilities Education Act (IDEA). These domains included

- physical development,
- cognitive development,
- language and speech development,
- psychosocial development, and
- self-help skills

(Public Law 99–457 1986).

For some time, the occupational therapists at the center had been writing occupational therapy reports according to the medical model. They questioned whether a new documentation form would enable them to provide parents, teachers, and caregivers with reports that were easier to understand. To evaluate the merits of this initiative, Helene and her colleagues decided to write a sample report. If pleased with the results, Helene and her staff would approach the team members at ABC Intermediate Unit and Family Service Program with their idea. Helene thought of Pierre, the child she met yesterday. Helene needed to start compiling the information she had collected in anticipation of writing a consultation report. The family and the day-care coordinator requested assistance to develop some strategies to prepare Pierre for school.

Helene Meets Pierre

Pierre is a 5-year-old child with Down's syndrome. He is monitored by the team at ABC, but he has not seen an occupational therapist for 6 months. When Helene arrives at the day-care center, both parents have taken the day off to meet with her. Pierre's parents are very proud of their only child and speak highly of his accomplishments.

Pierre appears to be one of the oldest and most active children at the day-care center. His aggressive play tendencies and verbal outbursts cannot be missed. He frequently attempts to direct other children's play, grabs toys from others, and refuses to share. Despite these interactions, Pierre has not learned the names of any of his playmates. His behavior is described as "destructive" by the day-care coordinator.

Pierre's egocentric tendencies work to his advantage in the personal care area. He will not let others help him with his shoes or coat and frequently says, "Pierre do it." When others attempt to assist, Pierre will say, "No," very forcefully. He is able to put on his shoes but cannot tie his laces. He puts on his coat with some assistance but cannot manage the zipper. He can put on his shirt but will often wear it backward or inside out. His mother indicates that his shoes are often on the wrong feet, if Pierre decides to wear them. She is pleased with his level of independence with personal care, and speaks proudly of these skills.

Pierre wears sweatpants and can manage these garments during toileting. He is not 100% toilet trained and frequently wets himself during rough outdoor play. Pierre's mother and the day-care coordinator take him to the toilet every hour for preventive purposes, and he wears a diaper to bed. During meals, Pierre eats most of his food with his fingers. His mother usually packs a sandwich and an apple for lunch. When the day-care center prepares other foods, Pierre refuses to eat or to use a utensil.

Books, construction activities, and gross motor play are Pierre's favorite activities. He spends hours looking at picture books and enjoys identifying different animals. He likes to build towers and buildings with large foam blocks but cannot stack more than three 1-inch blocks. On the playing field, Pierre loves playing ball but has little competency. He throws with gross accuracy but cannot catch or kick a moving ball. Pierre loves to sit on his tricycle and uses his feet on the ground for propulsion. His muscle tone is very low, and his joints are hypermobile.

When given single-inset puzzles, Pierre correctly matches simple shapes and forms. He refuses to string 1-inch beads, and his mother indicates that beads are too difficult for Pierre. Pierre refuses to practice cutting with children's scissors and dislikes crayons. He refuses to draw but enjoys painting. He has not established a hand dominance and uses a pronated fist grasp pattern with his paintbrush. Helene notices that most of his drawings are just collages of color.

The Challenge

You are Helene. Pierre's family and day-care coordinator have asked for your professional opinion regarding Pierre's readiness for school. What are your initial impressions? If you would like assistance with this challenge, use the questions and resources below to aid your analysis. Complete questions 2, 5–9 at a minimum.

Questions to Aid Analysis

1. What are the skills and abilities of a 5-year-old child? Can you classify these abilities into occupational performance areas and performance components using *Uniform Terminology* (American Occupational Therapy Association 1994), the CAOT position paper on pediatrics (Canadian Association of Occupational Therapists 1991), or using domains of developmental concern to the early intervention worker proposed by Tina, Helena's colleague?

2. What are the skills and abilities of this 5-year-old boy with Down's syndrome? Describe Pierre's independence in occupational performance areas, his skills and abilities in performance components, and the performance contexts of concern. Should you compare Pierre's performance to a typical 5-year-old child or evaluate him according to the expectations and competencies of a child with Down's syndrome?

3. What are the prevalence and features of mild, moderate, severe, and profound mental retardation? What are the differences among these categories?

4. What are some of the causative factors in mental retardation? What are the etiology and characteristics of Down's syndrome?

5. Using the information you have collected to date, begin to write your consultation report. Use the categories described in *Uniform Terminology* (American Occupational Therapy Association 1994), in the CAOT position paper (Canadian Association of Occupational Therapists 1991), or according to Tina's domains of developmental concern.

Table 4.2 Three Formats for Documenting Pediatric Occupational Therapy Services

	American Uniform Terminology (AOTA 1994)	Canadian Pediatric Position Paper (CAOT 1991)	Tina's Proposed Format
Performance Areas	Activities of daily living (ADL) Work and Productive activities Play or Leisure	Self-care Productivity Leisure	Education Self-help
Performance Components	Sensorimotor Cognitive integration and Cognitive components Psychosocial and Psychological	Motor Sensory integration Cognitive Psychological Social	Physical Cognitive Language and Speech Psychosocial
Performance Context	Temporal (Chronological, Developmental, Life Cycle, Disability Status) Environment (Physical, Social, Cultural)	Physical Social Cultural	

6. What standardized assessments of adaptive behavior could you use to establish a baseline against which progress and programming can be measured? Refer to Appendix A for assistance.

7. The family and day-care coordinator would like some specific suggestions regarding Pierre's social conduct. Write some measurable behavioral goals and objectives and include a time frame for achievement.

Goal 1: Pierre will be able to identify one friend by name without prompting within 1 month.

Objective 1a: Pierre will identify Bob by name with one or two verbal cues within 2 weeks.

Objective 1b:

Objective 1c:

Goal 2:

Objective 2a:

Objective 2b:

Objective 2c:

Goal 3:

Objective 3a:

Objective 3b:

Objective 3c:

8. Occupational therapists use many frames of reference to guide their thoughts during evaluation and intervention. Which approaches do you feel would be appropriate in Pierre's case?

9. Therapists frequently use the behavioral approach to guide services for children with mental retardation. Intervention focuses on modifying behaviors through shaping, fading, reinforcement, and punishment. Using this approach alone is ineffective, as skill maintenance and generalization are very difficult for the child with mental retardation. Identify some strategies that would promote skill maintenance and generalization.

10. Describe the process of continuous quality improvement (CQI). How is it the same/different than total quality management (TQM)?

New Terminology

continuous quality improvement	ICD-10	severe retardation
CQI	mental retardation	total quality management
Down's syndrome	mild retardation	TQM
DSM-IV	moderate retardation	trisomy 21
	profound retardation	

Learning Resources

American Occupational Therapy Association. 1994. Uniform terminology for occupational therapy, 3d ed. *American Journal of Occupational Therapy* 48:1047–1154.

American Occupational Therapy Association. 1994. Uniform terminology for occupational therapy, 3d ed. Application to practice. *American Journal of Occupational Therapy* 48:1055–59.

Acquaviva, J. D. 1992. *Effective documentation for occupational therapy.* Bethesda, MD: American Occupational Therapy Association.

Borst, M. J., and D. L. Nelson. 1993. Use of uniform terminology by occupational therapists. *American Journal of Occupational Therapy* 47:611–18.

Canadian Association of Occupational Therapists. 1990. *Position paper of occupational therapy in schools.* Toronto: Canadian Association of Occupational Therapists.

Canadian Association of Occupational Therapists. 1991. *Position paper on the role of occupational therapy in paediatrics.* Toronto: Canadian Association of Occupational Therapists.

Canadian Department of National Health and Welfare and Canadian Association of Occupational Therapists. 1983. *Guidelines for the client-centred practice of occupational therapy.* Ottawa, Ontario: Canadian Department of National Health and Welfare and Canadian Association of Occupational Therapists.

Kettenbach, G. 1990. *Writing S.O.A.P. notes.* Philadelphia: F. A. Davis.

McClain, L. 1991. Documentation. In *Pediatric occupational therapy: Facilitating effective service provision,* edited by W. Dunn, 213–44. Thorofare, NJ: Slack.

Watson, D. 1992. Documentation of paediatric assessments using occupational therapy guidelines for client-centred practice. *Canadian Journal of Occupational Therapy* 59:87–94.

Focus on Research

The estimated prevalence of mental retardation ranges from 10 to 30 per 1000 and differs in degree of severity (Gortmaker and Sappenfeld 1984). *Mental retardation* is defined as significant subaverage general intellectual functioning, as demonstrated by an intelligence quotient (IQ) of 70 or below on an individually administered IQ test, concurrent significant deficits or impairments in adaptive functioning, and onset before the age of 18 years (American Psychiatric Association 1994). *Adaptive functioning* refers to an individual's effectiveness in meeting the standards expected for age and by cultural group in at least two of the following skill areas: communication, self-care, home living, social/interpersonal skills, use of community resources, self-direction, functional academic skills, work, leisure, and health and safety (American Psychiatric Association 1994).

Although mental retardation is a medical diagnosis, it can occur in tandem with or as a secondary manifestation of another primary diagnosis (Kaplan et al. 1994).

The *Diagnostic and Statistical Manual* (DSM-IV)(American Psychiatric Association 1994) and *ICD-10 Classification of Mental and Behavioral Disorders* (World Health Organization 1992) classify individuals with mental retardation according to the severity (mild, moderate, severe, and profound) of the impairment in intellectual functioning. The educational model classifies children as either *educable* or *trainable*. These two terms are roughly equivalent to *mild* and *moderate* retardation (Crnic and Reid 1989). Parents of children with mental retardation are at risk for depression, emotional distress, social isolation, and reduced satisfaction from parenting. The family system also is at greater risk for dysfunction, including lack of cohesiveness and disharmony (Kaplan et al. 1994).

References

American Occupational Therapy Association. 1979. *Uniform terminology for reporting occupational therapy services.* Rockville, MD: American Occupational Therapy Association.

American Occupational Therapy Association. 1986. Guidelines for occupational therapy documentation. *American Journal of Occupational Therapy* 40:830–32.

American Occupational Therapy Association. 1989. Uniform terminology for occupational therapy, 2d ed. *American Journal of Occupational Therapy* 43:808–15.

American Occupational Therapy Association. 1994. Uniform terminology for occupational therapy, 3d ed. *American Journal of Occupational Therapy* 48:1047–54.

American Psychiatric Association. 1994. *Diagnostic and statistical manual of mental disorders, 4th ed.* Washington, D.C: American Psychiatric Association.

Canadian Association of Occupational Therapists. 1991. *Position paper on the role of occupational therapy in paediatrics.* Toronto: Canadian Association of Occupational Therapists.

Canadian Department of National Health and Welfare and Canadian Association of Occupational Therapists. 1983. *Guidelines for the client-centred practice of occupational therapy.* Ottawa, Ontario: Canadian Department of National Health and Welfare and Canadian Association of Occupational Therapists.

Crnic, K. A., and M. Reid. 1989. Mental retardation. In *Treatment of childhood disorders,* edited by E. J. Mash and R. A. Barkley. New York: Guilford.

Gortmaker, S. L., and W. Sappenfeld. 1984. Chronic childhood disorders: Prevalence and impact. *Pediatric Clinics of North America* 31:5.

Kaplan, H. I., B. J. Sadock, and J. A. Grebb. 1994. *Synopsis of psychiatry: Behavioral sciences and clinical psychiatry, 7th ed.* Baltimore: Williams & Wilkins.

U.S. House of Representatives. 1990. *Individuals with disabilities education act.* Public Law 101–476. Washington, D.C.

World Health Organization. 1992. *ICD-10 classification of mental and behavioral disorders: Clinical descriptions and diagnostic guidelines.* Geneva, Switzerland.

Module 5

Middle Childhood Cases

	Heidi	Tim (Part 1)	Tim (Part 2)	Robert	Gail
PBL Approach	Case method	Case method	Vignette	Case method	Case method
Age	6 years 7 months	6 years 7 months	6 years 9 months	8 years 1 month	10-year-old girl 6-year-old boy
Primary Diagnosis	Spina bifida	Undetermined learning difficulties	Undetermined learning difficulties	Traumatic brain injury	Cerebral palsy Traumatic brain injury
Area of Practice	Screening	Screening	Program planning	Program planning	Orthotic design
Location of Practice	Outpatient clinic	School	School	Rehabilitation center	Outpatient clinic
Frame of Reference	Human occupation and Visual perception	Human occupation and Sensory integration	Sensory integration	Human occupation Visual perception	Biomechanical
Performance Area	Self-help Education Leisure	Self-help Education Leisure	Self-help Education Leisure	Self-help Education Work Leisure	Education Leisure
Performance Components	Perceptual motor Psychosocial	Sensorimotor Cognitive Psychological Psychosocial	Sensorimotor	Sensorimotor Perceptual motor	Sensorimotor
Performance Context	Home and School	Physical and Social Environment	Physical and Social Environment	Social Environment	Physical Environment
Clinical Issues	Conflicting goals Documentation	Caseload management	Selecting therapeutic activities	Family teaching Prioritizing goals and objectives	Research evaluation and Continuing education
Occupational Therapy Tests	TVPS-R TVMS	COMPS Questionnaires Sensory Profile	SIPT	Clinical observations COAT MVPT-R VMI-R	Goniometer and Spasticity assessment

Children's Orientation and Amnesia Test (COAT); Clinical Observations of Motor and Postural Skills (COMPS); Motor-free Visual Perceptual Test-Revised (MVPT-R); Sensory Integration and Praxis Test (SIPT); Test of Visual Motor Skills (TVMS-R); Test of Visual Perceptual Skills (TVPS); Visual Motor Integration, 3rd ed., (VMI-R).

Middle Childhood Clinical Cases

Heidi

If there is anything that we wish to change in the child,
we must first examine it and see whether it is not
something that could better be changed in ourselves. *

—C.G. Jung

Background

After seeing three children, Stéphane returned from Spina Bifida Clinic. She sat at her desk preparing to write her occupational therapy (OT) report and wondered how much detail to include. The clinic's pediatric neurologist was always looking for a thorough, concise report that focused on function. Stéphane wondered if she could incorporate some of the techniques suggested at a workshop she attended last week on documentation.

Spina Bifida Clinic was established at ABC Rehabilitation Center to provide coordinated and comprehensive evaluation and treatment to children with congenital spinal cord anomalies. The clinic monitored all children with spina bifida regularly, but Stéphane focused her attention on children with meningomyelocele, which occurs in 94% of spina bifida cystica cases (Menelaus 1980).

Heidi, 6 years 7 months, had been diagnosed at birth with a lumbar (L1/L2) meningomyelocele and received a shunt for hydrocephalus. When she was 2 years old, mother complained of "unusual eating habits," as Heidi only chewed food with her front teeth. Heidi skillfully removed the skin from peas with her front teeth and swallowed only the pulp. The occupational therapist brought this observation to the attention of the clinic's neurologist, who performed a thorough workup. Heidi underwent cranial surgery for posterior fossa decompression. When Heidi was reassessed by an occupational therapist at age 3, Heidi's family did not express any concerns or identify any functional problems. An assessment of fine motor proficiency and preschool skills was performed for preventative measures, but the results were within normal ranges.

---

*Jung, C. G. 1939. *The Integration of the Personality.* Reprinted with permission from Princeton University Press.

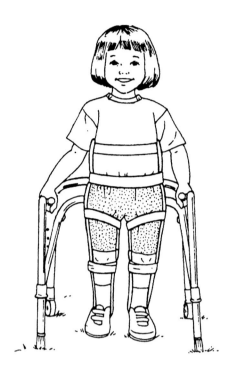

Figure 5.1 Heidi with Hip-Knee-Ankle Brace

Stéphane spoke with Heidi's school teacher, Ms. R., 2 days ago. The local school district contracted therapy services from ABC Rehabilitation Center, and Heidi's mother signed a consent form allowing the school to discuss Heidi's performance with the clinic team members.

Ms. R. indicated that there were two children with disabilities in her class of 30 and only one teaching assistant. "Naturally, Heidi receives all the attention she needs from us. . . She is a very lovely child, and we like to help her out in our classroom. The kids are great with her, as she always has something to say. Sometimes, however, she doesn't wait her turn to speak. . . Her paper work is messy, but good printing will not become important until at least third grade. Besides, people can hardly read my handwriting, either."

Stéphane decided to pursue more specifics, as she knew that many children with meningomyelocele were at risk for speech, perceptual, and motor problems that could impact on school performance. Stéphane asked, "Specifically what type of help does your assistant provide?"

Ms. R. indicated that her assistant always accompanies Heidi to the bathroom and helps at lunchtime. At gym time and recess, the assistant sits with Heidi.

Further discussions revealed that although Heidi had a hip, knee, and ankle gait orthosis, this device had never been brought to school. After answering questions about Heidi's accomplishments for the year, Ms. R. said that Heidi would graduate into second grade. She added that Heidi could print the *H, i,* and *d,* but printing the *e* was difficult for her. Ms. R. reported asking Heidi's mother to practice printing with Heidi during the summer. When asked about math and science concepts, the teacher summarized Heidi's progress as "a little slow in math" with "no problems" in science. Stéphane indicated she would be visiting with Heidi's family soon and asked if Ms. R. would welcome a school visit. Ms. R. said a visit would be fine.

Stéphane Meets Heidi

Heidi is seen with her mother and 3-year-old brother, George. The occupational therapy screening is scheduled for 45 minutes because Heidi also has appointments with physical therapy, nursing, and the clinic's neurologist. When Stéphane, her occupational therapist, walks into the waiting room, she notices that Heidi is sitting in a wheelchair (w/ c) that appears to fit well and is in good repair. However, Heidi is sitting on a towel rather than a w/c cushion. Stéphane makes a mental note to bring this up later in the interview.

Stéphane carries two standardized tests with her to the clinic, the *Test of Visual Perceptual Skills* (non-motor) (TVPS) (Gardner 1982) and the *Test of Visual-Motor Skills-Revised* (TVMS-R) (Gardner 1995). Ms. R.'s comments make Stéphane wonder about Heidi's visual perceptual motor abilities. When they all reach the privacy of an evaluation room, Stéphane asks if the family has any concerns. Heidi is in high spirits and talks endlessly about her school and friends.

Mother: We were wondering about where to get a new wheelchair cushion.

Stéphane smiles, pleased that Heidi's mother has identified this issue, and proceeds to make some recommendations. As the interview continues, Stéphane asks about specific competencies in dressing, feeding, toilet training, bathing, w/c care and mobility, academic performance, leisure play, and community involvement. Interrater agreement between OT and parent assessments of the abilities of children with spina bifida in activities of daily living is greater than 85% (Unruh et al. 1993).

Mother: Heidi has been dressing herself for one year, but she continues to have difficulty with zippers, buttons smaller than one inch in diameter, snaps on overcoats and pants, and shoelaces. She uses a knife, fork, and spoon during meals.

George: She's so messy.

When asked about independence at school, it is revealed that Heidi is unable to peel an orange or banana. Tupperware containers and plastic self-sealing bags are also difficult. Heidi is unable to independently manage her bladder and bowel care.

Mother: She has simply never tried self-catheterization but must learn to do this before she is allowed to sleep over at her friend Anna's house. I lift her into the tub, and Heidi gives herself a bath.

Mother: *(When asked about school)* I'm concerned about academics. Heidi's teacher doesn't seem to have a problem with her performance. Heidi has to practice printing, particularly her first name. Shouldn't she be able to do this herself?

Stéphane: *(Being careful not to alarm Heidi's mother)* Most children at Heidi's age should be able to print their names. But some letters are harder to print than others; therefore, some words are harder to print. It will become very important in the second grade to be independent in this area. I brought along some tests that may give us an idea about what is causing this difficulty. Would you like to try them?

Heidi: Mom, tell her about swimming!

George: Ya.

Stéphane: Why don't you tell me about swimming?

Heidi: Well, see, I always liked swimming, and I even have a new suit. But I can't go because I am scared about something. I don't really like to watch, and George gets to go. He is even younger than I am. My friend, Anna, she goes too. She doesn't have a new suit, but she has a pretty yellow one. Yellow is a good color. I have a pretty yellow dress.

Stéphane: Heidi, let me ask you a few questions about this. Can you get into your bathing suit by yourself?

Heidi: Yes, if it is the blue one and I do it at home on my bed.

Stéphane: Once your wheelchair is put beside the pool, can you think of a way to get from your chair to the ground?

Mother: *(Shakes her head)* That is Heidi's main fear.

Heidi: That is the problem. I'm scared. I want to play in the water. I have a bright orange jacket. What if I fall? Mom will be mad.

Stéphane: If you learned how to do this, would you be able to go swimming without being scared?

Heidi: Yes, I am sure of it!

Stéphane: I think this is something we can work on, don't you?

George: Ya. *(Heidi and her mother agree.)*

Stéphane: Can we get back to doing the projects I brought for you, Heidi?

Heidi: Sure. I like tests. We have them at school all the time. Anna sits next to me, you know. She likes tests, too.

Stéphane starts with the TVPS (Gardner 1988). Heidi concentrates intently and looks at all the pictures presented. She takes between 7 to 10 seconds per picture on the subtest of visual spatial relations. During other subtests, she takes only 2 to 3 seconds. See Figure 5.2.

TEST OF VISUAL-PERCEPTUAL SKILLS (non-motor)
Morrison F. Gardner
Children's Hospital, San Francisco
Individual Record Form

Name: _Heidi_   Sex: _F_ Grade: _____

School: _____ Examiner: _Stéphane_

Date of Test: _____ _____ _____
                   year   month   day

Date of Birth: _____ _____ _____
                   year   month   day

Chronological Age: _6_ _7_ _____
                   year   month   day*

* If the number of days exceeds 15, consider as a full month and increase the months by one.

TEST RESULTS:	Raw Scores	Perceptual Ages	Scaled Scores	Percentile Ranks
Visual Discrimination	7			
Visual Memory	3			
Visual-Spatial Relationships	2			
Visual Form Constancy	5			
Visual Sequential Memory	1			
Visual Figure-Ground	2			
Visual Closure	4			

Sum of Scaled Scores: _____   *Percentile Rank:* _____

Perceptual Quotient: _____   *Median Perceptual Age:* _____

Figure 5.2 *Test of Visual-Perception Skills (non-motor)* Individual Record Form

Stéphane recites the instructions for the TVMS-R (Gardner 1995) and gives Heidi a copy of the test booklet. Heidi holds her pencil in her right hand with a static immature tripod grip and begins the test. The following illustrations are six samples of the 23 drawings made by Heidi. See Figures 5.3–5.8.

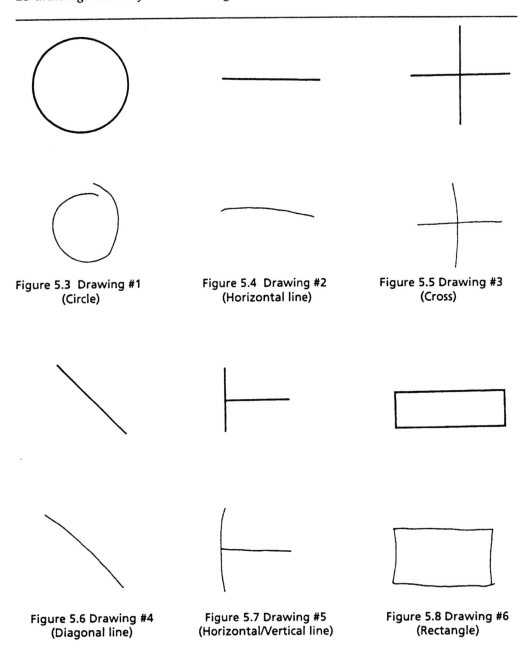

Figure 5.3 Drawing #1
(Circle)

Figure 5.4 Drawing #2
(Horizontal line)

Figure 5.5 Drawing #3
(Cross)

Figure 5.6 Drawing #4
(Diagonal line)

Figure 5.7 Drawing #5
(Horizontal/Vertical line)

Figure 5.8 Drawing #6
(Rectangle)

To conclude the screening session, Stéphane describes her telephone interview with Ms. R. and states her initial impressions. After the team conference, Stéphane will be able to call the family with the results from TVPS (Gardner 1988) and TVMS-R (Gardner 1995) and with any OT recommendations.

The Challenge

You are Stéphane, and you have just completed this screening session. Prepare for the team conference, and write your screening report. If you would like assistance with this challenge, use the questions and resources below to aid your analysis. Complete questions 1, 3, 5-9, 12, 13, 15, and 17 at a minimum. See Appendix E for Selected Answers.

Questions to Aid Analysis

1. What is spina bifida? Describe its etiology and the different types. Why does Stéphane spend a lot of time with children with meningomyelocele?

2. Why do so many children with spina bifida require shunts? What are the clinical signs and symptoms of shunt malfunction in infants, toddlers, and school-aged children? (Refer to Tappit-Emas 1994.)

3. What are the roles, tasks, and activities of a 6-year 7-month-old child? Can you classify these abilities into occupational performance areas: self-care, productive work, and leisure play?

4. Describe the developmental stage of middle childhood according to Erik Erikson and Robert Havighurst. What do these theorists tell you about Heidi's development?

5. Describe Heidi's volitional (personal causation, interests, and values), habituation (habits, patterns, and roles), and performance subsystems. Does this occupational profile promote health, well-being, and personal satisfaction?

6. How does environmental context (physical, social, and cultural) affect Heidi's independence?

7. Finish scoring the TVPS (Gardner 1988). Complete the Individual Record Form (Figure 5.2) and TVPS Profile Chart (Figure 5.9). What do the scaled scores and perceptual quotient tell you about Heidi's performance. See Appendix D.

Practice using the manual and scoring criteria to classify Heidi's errors (weaknesses) and accuracy (strengths) using the sample of six illustrations provided (Figures 5.3–5.8). Compare your results with those provided in Appendix D.

Finish scoring the TVMS-R (Gardner 1995) Test Profile using the test manual. Convert the Total Accurate Raw Score to a motor age, standard and scaled score, percentile rank, and stanine. What do these results tell you about Heidi's visual-motor accuracy? See Figure 5.10. See Appendix D for assistance with this exercise.

%tile Rank	VD	VM	VSR	VFC	VSM	VFG	VC	%tile Rank
99.9	19	19	19	19	19	19	19	99.9
99.6	18	18	18	18	18	18	18	99.6
99	17	17	17	17	17	17	17	99
98	16	16	16	16	16	16	16	98
95	15	15	15	15	15	15	15	95
91	14	14	14	14	14	14	14	91
84	13	13	13	13	13	13	13	84
75	12	12	12	12	12	12	12	75
63	11	11	11	11	11	11	11	63
50	10	10	10	10	10	10	10	50
37	9	9	9	9	9	9	9	37
25	8	8	8	8	8	8	8	25
16	7	7	7	7	7	7	7	16
9	6	6	6	6	6	6	6	9
5	5	5	5	5	5	5	5	5
2	4	4	4	4	4	4	4	2
1	3	3	3	3	3	3	3	1
0.4	2	2	2	2	2	2	2	0.4
0.1	1	1	1	1	1	1	1	0.1

TVPS Profile Chart (Scaled Scores)

Use for charting a child's visual-perceptual areas of functioning based on scaled scores.

Figure 5.9 TVPS Profile Chart

Test of Visual-Motor Skills-Revised

Morrison F. Gardner

Scoring Criterion Booklet

Name: _Heidi_   Sex: _F_   Grade: _1_

School: _____ Examiner: _Stephane_

Hand: R _✓_   L _____

Prehension of Pencil: _static immature tripod._

Date of Test: _____ _____ _____
            year   month   day

Date of Birth: _____ _____ _____
            year   month   day

Chronological Age: _6_ _7_ _____
            year   month   day*

* If the number of days exceeds 15, consider as a full month and increase the months by one.

TEST PROFILE

Test Results:

Accurate (One) Characteristics

Total Accurate Raw Score _71_   Motor Age _____

Standard Score _____   Scaled Score _____   Percentile Rank _____   Stanine _____

Error (Zero) Characteristics

Classifications	Total Error Raw Scores	Standard Scores	Scaled Scores	Percentile Ranks	Stanines
(1)	6				
(2)	25				
(3)	11				
(4)	5				
(5)	7				
(6)	7				
(7)	6				
(8)	9				

Figure 5.10 *Test of Visual-Motor Skills-Revised* Scoring Criterion Booklet

Stéphane has scored all 23 test illustrations and determined the Total Error Raw Scores. Use these figures to determine the standard and scaled scores, percentile ranks, and stanines for each of the following eight error classifications (See Figure 5.10):

- Closure
- Angles
- Intersecting and/or Overlapping individual lines
- Size of form or Part of form
- Rotation or Reversal
- Line Length
- Overpenetration or Underpenetration
- Modification of form

(Gardner 1995, 23)

What do these results tell you about Heidi's visual-motor strengths and limitations? Do these findings relate to any of the results obtained on the TVPS (Gardner 1988)?

Become familiar with the Pediatric Evaluation of Disability Inventory *(PEDI) (Haley et al. 1989) and the* Functional Independence Measure for children *(Wee FIM) (Granger and Hamilton 1992). The PEDI will give you an appreciation for the age ranges during which children master self-care, mobility, and social skills (Haley et al. 1992, Table 3.8, 3.9, 3.10 and 3.11, pp. 30–40).*

The testing information contained within this case has been included so that you may become familiar with TVPS (Gardner 1988) and TVMS-R (Gardner 1995). However, practice apprenticeship is required for test administration and interpretation competency.

8. How will Heidi's strengths and abilities affect her weaknesses and disabilities?

9. How can you use the model of human occupation or the visual-perceptual frame of reference to guide your evaluation and recommendations?

10. Assume that you had access to Heidi's psychological test results measuring intelligence. If her scores placed her intellectual abilities one standard deviation below the mean, would this influence the significance of your test results? Heidi's intelligence quotient (IQ) scores, however, place her performance at the mean. How does this influence your impressions regarding her visual perceptual motor skills and occupational performance?

11. Complete the following chart by delineating both this family's and your concerns regarding Heidi's performance, the performance components and contexts that impact them, and finally about some behavioral observations supporting these claims. The *Uniform Terminology for Occupational Therapy* document from the American Occupational Therapy Association (1994) provides a taxonomy system that will assist you in this process. By documenting behavioral evidence, you can more easily define measurable and objective outcome indicators.

Occupational Performance Area Concerns (Self-Care, Productive Work and Leisure)	Contributory Performance Components and Contexts	Supporting Behavioral Observations

12. What do you expect Heidi's goals are for herself? What about Mother? George? Heidi's current teacher? What about Heidi's teacher for next year? Given this, along with your test results and clinical observations, what are your goals to maintain or promote function, and to prevent dysfunction?

   Goal #1

   Goal #2

   Goal #3

   Goal #4

   Goal #5

13. Have you identified any areas of dysfunction that do not appear to be an issue with the teacher or family? If so, what will you do?

14. Which w/c cushion would you recommend? Not every cushion will meet Heidi's needs. When recommending cushion options, consider Heidi's diagnosis, clinical symptomatology, body build, lifestyle, method and frequency of transfers, activity level, and climate. There are a number of cushion designs on the market today that basically fit into one of six categories (see the following chart).

	Air-Filled	Gel Flotation	Polymer Foam
Custom			
Commercial			

Air-filled cushions are available in different widths, depths, and heights. They are cool, lightweight, and easily cleaned but require good balance and maintenance. Gel flotation cushions provide good pressure relief and are easy to clean, but they are heavy and may freeze in harsh winter climates. Polymer foam cushions are the most popular and are affordable. They are lightweight and available in different densities to meet body position and body-weight needs. Foam may be shaped to fit individual needs. Cloth covers maximize the pressure relief properties of the foam, while vinyl covers protect against incontinence or exposure to liquids.

15. What other professional(s) should Heidi see during her visit to your clinic? Should you recommend that Heidi receive OT services? Where? How often?

16. Now that you have had exposure to the report writing styles presented in the *Antonio* and *Pierre* cases, write your own screening report.

17. It's time for a conference, and you will have about 2 minutes to share your findings with the team. Be prepared to summarize your results and to state your recommendations within this time frame.

New Terminology

apnea	immature static tripod	standard deviation
Arnold Chiari	lipoma	standard score
diastematomyelia	meningocele	stanine
filum terminale	meningomyelocele	strabismus
gastroesophageal reflux	retrocollis	stridor
hydrocephalus	scoliosis	tethered cord
hydromyelia	shunt	ventriculo-peritoneal (V-P) shunt

Learning Resources

Information on the TVPS (Gardner 1988)and TVMS-R (Gardner 1995) is provided in Appendix A. Canadian readers should use the uniform terminology proposed in the Client-Centred Model of Occupational Performance (Canadian Association of Occupational Therapists 1983) outlined in Appendix C.

American Occupational Therapy Association. 1994. Uniform terminology for occupational therapy, 3d ed. *American Journal of Occupational Therapy* 48:1047–54.

Chow, B., and P. Volpe. 1993. *Visual perceptual development and remedial activities: Set II.* Burlingame, CA: Psychological and Educational Publications.

Gardner Codding, K., and M. F. Gardner. 1987. *Visual-motor development: Remedial activities.* Burlingame, CA: Psychological and Educational Publications, Inc.

Tappit-Emas, E. 1994. *Pediatric Physical Therapy, 2d ed.*, edited by J. Stephen Tecklin, 135–86. Philadelphia: J. B. Lippincott.

Watson, D. 1991. Occupational therapy intervention guidelines for children and adolescents with spina bifida. *Child: Care, health and development* 17:367–80.

Wheelchair cushions may be evaluated by reviewing medical supplier catalogs. Contact information for two manufacturers follows:

Roho, Incorporated
100 Florida Avenue
Belleville, IL 62221-5430
1-800-851-3449

Jay Medical Ltd.
P.O. Box 18656
Boulder, CO 80308-8656
1-800-648-8282

Focus on Research

Although the incidence of spina bifida in the United States decreased from 5.2/10,000 live births in 1980 to 4.3/10,000 in 1987, it is the most common and disabling birth defect and major contributor to morbidity and mortality in childhood. Annual medical and surgical care costs for all persons with spina bifida in the United States probably exceed $200 million (Public Health Service 1989). Canadian incidence in British Columbia residents, between 1952 and 1986 inclusively, is 3.7/10,000 live births (Bamforth and Baird 1989). Although specific causes are not known, both genetic and environmental factors play an interactive role.

The most obvious clinical features of meningomyelocele include motor impairment, orthopedic deformities, loss of sensation, and loss of genitourinary control. Tethered cord, hydrocephalus, and Chiari II malformation place the child at risk for future neurological complications. Oculomotor irregularities and upper-extremity movement anomalies are common. Orthopedic deformities, due to scattered innervation or agenesis, may be present at birth or progressive. Concurrent anomalies, such as a thickened filum terminale, diastematomyelia, hydromyelia, or lipoma, may cause tethering, where deterioration of motor or sensory function, progressive scoliosis, changes in urological status, and back or leg pain are possible (Boop et al. 1992). Monitoring and identifying early changes in neurological status are critical.

The Arnold-Chiari malformation, specifically Chiari II, is almost always evident and may be associated with apnea, stridor, vocal cord paralysis, gastroesophageal reflux, hyperactive gag reflex, retrocollis, nystagmus, upper body weakness, hypotonia or spasticity, and feeding difficulties (McCullough 1986; Stark 1977). Strabismus is evident 42% to 59% of the time (Hunt 1981; Turner 1985). Obstruction by the Chiari II is the most common cause of hydrocephalus in children with spina bifida. Hydrocephalus occurs in 70% to 86% of cases and may cause motor, intellectual, language, and perceptual dysfunction (Hunt 1981; Knowlton et al. 1985). The term *cocktail party speech* is used to describe the hyperverbal behavior in children with spina bifida and hydrocephalus (Schwartz 1974).

Current prognosis for children with high meningomyelocele, in terms of functional skills as adults, is poor, as they rarely maintain competitive employment, and only 50% (approximately) achieve independent living status (Hinderer et al. 1988). Recent changes in the Americans with Disabilities Act and Individuals with Disabilities Education Act address these issues.

References

Bamforth, S. J., and P. A. Baird. 1989. Spina bifida and hydrocephalus: A population study over a 35-year period. *American Journal of Human Genetics* 44 (February):225–32.

Boop, F. A., A. Russell, and W. M. Chadduck. 1992. Diagnosis and management of the tethered cord syndrome. *Journal of Arkansas Medical Society* 89(December):328–31.

Gardner, M. F. 1982. *Test of visual perceptual skills.* Burlingame, CA: Psychological and Educational Publications.

Gardner, M. F. 1995. *Test of visual motor skills-revised.* Burlingame, CA: Psychological and Educational Publications.

Granger, C. V., and B. B. Hamilton. 1992. *Functional Independence Measure for Children* (WeeFim). Buffalo, NY: UDS Data Management Service.

Haley, S., et al. 1989. *Pediatric Evaluation of Disability Inventory* (PEDI). Boston: PEDI Research Group.

Hinderer, S. R., K. A. Hinderer, K. Dunne, and D. B. Shurtleff. 1988. Medical and functional status of adults with spina bifida. *Developmental Medicine and Child Neurology* (Supplement) 57:28.

Hunt, G. M. 1981. Spina bifida: Implications for 100 children at school. *Developmental Medicine and Child Neurology* 23:160–72.

Knowlton, D. D., K. Peterson, and A. Putbrese. 1985. Team management of cognitive dysfunction in children with spina bifida. *Rehabilitation Literature* 46:259–63.

McCullough, D. C. 1986. Theories of development of the Arnold Chiari malformation. In *Spina bifida: A multidisciplinary approach,* edited by R. L. McLaurin, S. Oppenheimer, L. Dias, and W. E. Kaplan, New York: Praeger, 159–63.

Menelaus, M. 1980. *The orthopaedic management of spina bifida cystica.* 2d ed. New York: Churchill Livingstone.

Public Health Service, Center for Disease Control. 1989. Economic burden of spina bifida—United States, 1980–1990. *Morbidity and Mortality Weekly Report* 38:264–67.

Schwartz, E. 1974. Characteristics of speech and language development in children with myelomeningocele and hydrocephalus. *Journal of Speech and Hearing Disorders* 39:465–68.

Stark, G. D. 1977. *Spina bifida: Problems and management.* Boston: Blackwell Scientific.

Turner, A. 1985. Hand function in children with myelomeningocele. *Journal of Bone and Joint Surgery* 67-B:268–72.

Unruh, A. M., S. Fairchild, and J. Versnel. 1993. Parents' and therapists' ratings of self care skills in children with spina bifida. *Canadian Journal of Occupational Therapy* 60:145.

Tim (Part 1)

It is doubtful that any child may reasonably be expected to succeed in life if he is denied the opportunity of an education. Such an opportunity, where the state has undertaken to provide it, is a right which must be made available to all on equal terms.

—Brown v. Board of Education,
United States Supreme Court, 1954

Background

In 1990, 18.6% of occupational therapists and 17% of certified occupational therapy assistants in the United States worked within the school system (American Occupational Therapy Association 1991). Most school-based therapists work directly for the school district on a full-time basis rather than on a contractual basis (Chandler 1994a). Since late July, Meredith has worked as an occupational therapist at ABC School District (ABCSD), a rural community with 20 small schools. She was the first and only staff therapist. Prior to her arrival, ABCSD contracted services on an as-needed basis. ABCSD administrators indicated that Meredith's predecessors had spent the last two years on student needs assessments and staff education.

Meredith had begun to assemble a policy and procedures manual for therapy services and was working to define the process of referral, evaluation, program planning, service provision, documentation, and program evaluation. The occupational therapy referral policy had to comply with ABCSD, state, and federal policies, regulations, and mandates. The evaluation process included screening, evaluation, and periodic reviews, and program planning required collaboration with team members to develop an Individualized Educational Plan (IEP). Occupational therapy service provision could include any combination of direct service; case, colleague, parent, or system consultation; monitoring; and referral for other services (Dunn 1991). Meredith expected that her documentation time allotment would be computed on a 1:4 ratio—1 hour of preparation and documentation for every 4 hours spent with students (American Occupational Therapy Association 1989).

In anticipation of preparing her first annual report, Meredith intended to proactively track the type and scope of her occupational therapy services, the impact of intervention, and her professional development efforts to evaluate service quality. Meredith had been informed that most of her funding was from federal and state government sources. ABCSD paid the remainder of her financial endowment to ensure that therapists spend their time seeing the children, providing holistic services, and helping the teachers. The Education for All Handicapped Children Act (P.L. 94–142), renamed the Individuals with Disabilities Education Act (IDEA) (P.L. 101–476) in 1990, identified occupational therapy as a related service that may be provided to help children with disabilities benefit from special education.

In early October, Meredith received a call from Mr. L., a new elementary school teacher. Mr. L. seemed anxious to share his impressions about Tim, one of his students. "This boy is very inattentive. He is a behavior problem! He is so active; I wonder if he is listening. His psychoeducational testing revealed average intelligence, but I think something is wrong. He never finishes any class projects, and he is so clumsy. He still can't print his name. I'll burn out by December."

Meredith interviewed Mr. L., spent some time observing Tim in the classroom, and obtained completed questionnaires from Mr. L. and Tim's family. Ninety-five percent of school-based occupational therapists use classroom observation as an assessment procedure; 85% interview teachers; and 72% observe students in school environments outside of the classroom (Chandler 1994b).

When Meredith began her new position, she reviewed the literature to locate parent or teacher questionnaires that assessed occupational performance competencies and sensorimotor development. Although a number of questionnaires attempted to detect students with sensory processing problems by identifying distinguishing behaviors, these typically addressed only the tactile system (Royeen 1987; Royeen and Fortune 1990) or had very little research to substantiate the items chosen. Meredith decided she would design a questionnaire that required parents to identify their child's strengths, weaknesses, and special learning needs. She also designed a Sensory Profile (Figure 5.12) to give to parents whose children demonstrated signs of sensory-integrative dysfunction. Her profile was based on research published in the *American Journal of Occupational Therapy* (Dunn 1994) and on a sensory history questionnaire designed by Cook (1991). Meredith fashioned the Teacher Questionnaire (Figure 5.13) in the same manner and used some additional resources to compile a School Performance Profile (Figure 5.14) (American Psychiatric Association 1994; Individuals with Disabilities Education Act 1990).

Meredith Meets Tim

Tim is a 6-year 7-month-old boy who attends first grade. Mr. L., his teacher, admits having very little experience with challenging children.

Mr. L: Tim needs a special class and a teacher who has more experience at this sort of thing.

Students in this class are expected to independently organize their belongings upon arrival. Tim has difficulty getting his zipper undone and taking his coat off and eventually leaves his jacket, turned inside out, on the floor. The first class activity, circle time, lasts 15 minutes. The students sit together on the floor in a circle to determine the day of the week and the date to discuss the weather. One of the students presents an item for show-and-tell, and the children raise their hands to ask questions. On three occasions, Tim contributes information to the group without being asked.

Mr. L: *(Tim continually wants to lie on the floor)* Sit up like your friends.

The students return to their desks to complete a cut, color, and paste project that they started the day before. Tim leaves circle time with the other children but runs past his desk to the guinea pig cage in the corner. Mr. L. sees him trying to open the cage door and instructs Tim to return to his desk. While most of the children are completing their pumpkin project, Tim is trying to find his scissors, glue, and crayons. He pulls loose supplies and work sheets from his cluttered and haphazard desk shelf.

Tim: (*Noticing that part of his paper pumpkin is ripped*) Someone ruined my paper!

Mr. L.:   Slow down, Tim. Relax and count to 3. Then, we can start over.

Mr. L. goes to his desk, and obtains another pre-drawn picture.

Tim, why don't you cut out this new pumpkin?

Tim: But my scissors and glue are gone.

Tim seems to be missing most of his crayons and pencils and has apparently lost two lunch boxes since September. Mr. L. proceeds to help Tim get organized at his desk. Within a few minutes, Tim starts to cut the pumpkin design. He frequently drops his scissors and eventually stands at his desk and uses one hand to hold down the paper while he cuts. When he finds it too difficult to manipulate the scissors, he resorts to tearing the paper. Eventually, Tim places the eyes, nose, and mouth pieces on his project with excessive amounts of white glue. As he prints his name on the back of the pumpkin, the saturated paper starts to tear. Tim picks up pieces of wet paper pumpkin, rolls them into a ball, and throws them at his classmate.

Across the room, some of the children who have completed their project gather around a computer. As the program starts, the speakers begin to chime. Tim hears the music, goes over to join the crowd, and tries to push his way toward the keyboard. After the students tell him to leave, Tim ventures over to the construction corner. He picks up and manipulates small pieces of plastic building blocks but does not assemble any specific structure. For the next 5 minutes of free-play time, Tim moves around the room to various workstations and watches his classmates.

When the children are recalled to their desks for journal time, Tim is the last to be seated. Mr. L. has arranged the desks in small groups of four. The desks have one open shelf underneath the tabletop, and the children are expected to organize and care for their own supplies. Tim's chair seems a bit too big for him. He constantly squirms in his seat and wraps his legs around the chair or desk posts. On a number of occasions, he pushes the chair back to enable himself to stand at his desk. On two occasions, he loses his balance and slips off his seat onto the floor. Tim is unable to independently pull the chair forward to the table edge from a sitting position, and his classmate helps him with this task twice. By not sitting close to the table, Tim repeatedly drops important project pieces or utensils onto the floor.

Tim: I'm too tired to work.

Once the journals are distributed, the children are expected to copy the date and three new words from the board and to draw a picture. All children are required to print their name on the top right-hand corner of their page. Mr. L. prints Tim's name and the date on his paper.

Mr. L: I want you to use your pencil to trace over your name. Then, do your best copying the words from the board.

By the end of journal time, Tim has drawn unrecognizable pictures on his booklet. As the recess bell rings, Mr. L. helps Tim into his overcoat.

Mr. L: *(During an interview)* Tim plays with everyone during recess. He doesn't play with anyone very long, unless they are playing soccer. Tim loves soccer; he runs endlessly trying to make a play but trips over the ball every time he gets the opportunity to kick it. Yesterday, he made a few enemies at the slide by refusing to wait in line as the others did. The students would not let him in line, so he tried climbing up from the bottom of the slide and caused an accident. A few of the children avoid playing with him.

When asked about gym time, Mr. L. continues.

Tim finishes the obstacle course first but inevitably avoids the balance activities, and he frequently trips. He throws a ball well but doesn't like to catch.

During recess, Meredith spends about 5 minutes with Tim and three of his classmates. She engages them in a game of imitating postures in order to gain more information about Tim.

Meredith: Put your hands on your head. Can you stand on one foot?

Tim assumes a rather contorted posture and is unable to maintain his position for more than 3 or 4 seconds, while his classmates stand like statues for at least 10 seconds. As Meredith continues with these verbal commands, Tim watches all of the other children and performs well. When she challenges the children to imitate her position, Tim has great difficulty planning his movement and positioning himself. To complete the game, Meredith challenges each child to walk the length of a curb without falling off. One of the children completes the activity gracefully. Two of the children require some assistance but are able to complete the task. Tim insists that Meredith hold his hand.

Tim: *(Walking along the curb and swaying back and forth)* The alligators down there are ready to eat me.

It is Meredith's impression that Tim has created this story to hide the fact that he finds the task difficult.

Meredith returned to Tim's school in one week to pick up the completed Parent and Teacher Questionnaires and to administer the Clinical Observation of Motor and Postural Skills *(COMPS), Appendix A. The COMPS is a standardized assessment that is used to screen motor coordination problems (Wilson et al. 1994). Tim is eager to try all of the tasks and often starts activities before the instructions or demonstrations are complete. After administering this screening test, Meredith discusses therapy services with Tim. (See COMPS Scoring Sheet, Figure 5.15.)*

Meredith: Do you think that there are activities that you may need some help with?

Tim:　　No, not really.

Meredith: Do you remember when I came to your class last week?

Tim:　　Sure. I remember everything.

Meredith: During journal time, it seemed to me that you had difficulty printing and concentrating on your work. Is that right?

Tim:　　Yes, printing is very hard. I can't do it. I try hard, and Mom says that's important.

Meredith: That is very important. Would you like some help learning to concentrate and practicing your printing?

Tim:　　That would be good. Could you help me learn to play soccer, too?

Meredith: We will certainly see if that is possible.

On the way back to class, Tim comments on other students' art work and projects displayed in the halls. Tim greets everyone who passes by and knows many of the children's names. Before Meredith leaves, Mr. L. mentions that he has scheduled an IEP meeting and will be meeting with Meredith the following day. See the completed Parent Questionnaire, Sensory Profile, Teacher Questionnaire, School Performance Profile, and COMPS Scoring Sheet that follow (Figures 5.11–5.15).

Date: *October 15*

Child's Information:

Name: *Tim*   **Date of Birth:** *3/15*

Family Information:

Father's Name: *B. Tim's father does not live with us. He never understood Tim!*

Occupation: *Carpenter*

Mother's Name: *R.*

Occupation: *Homemaker*

Names and ages of brothers and/or sisters: *None*

Describe your child's strengths and weaknesses, then rank them in order of their importance (1 = most important; 5 = least important).

Strengths	Rank	Weaknesses	Rank
Interested in many things	*3*	*Doesn't concentrate*	*2*
Friendly with all children	*4*	*Clumsy*	*1*
Loves books	*5*	*Interested in too many things*	*3*
Kind	*1*		
Proud	*2*		

I don't want my child in a special class or to see any more doctors.

Please complete the following questions to enable us to better understand your child.

In your opinion, does your child require special services to enable him/her to benefit from their educational program. If so, why?

Yes, I suppose he needs help to learn to print.

Has your child been diagnosed with a condition that would justify the need for special education services?

No.

Has your child had an eye evaluation?

Yes, by our family doctor, Dr. K., 3 years ago because Tim falls a lot and can't find things. His eyes are good. It's a concentration problem.

Has your child had a hearing evaluation?

Yes, he is good. He had a lot of ear infections until he was about 3.

Is your child currently on any medication?

No

Figure 5.11 Parent Questionnaire

Sensory Profile

Complete the following observation checklist by rating your child 1 through 5. Select and circle the number that best describes your child.	1 Always 100% of the time	2 Fre- quently 75% of the time	3 Occasion- ally 50% of the time	4 Seldom 25% of the time	5 Never 0% of the time
Auditory					
Responds negatively to unexpected or loud noises	1	②	3	4	5
Holds hands over ears	1	2	3	4	⑤
Can't work with background noise	①	2	3	4	5
Visual					
Hesitates going up or down curbs or steps	1	2	3	4	⑤
Gets lost easily	1	②	3	4	5
Doesn't notice when people come into the room	1	2	3	4	⑤
Taste/Smell					
Chews/licks on nonfood objects	1	2	3	4	⑤
Does not seem to smell strong odors	1	2	3	④	5
Movement					
Avoids climbing, jumping, bumpy or uneven ground	1	②	3	4	5
Avoids playground equipment or moving toys	1	2	③	4	5
Holds onto walls or banisters	1	2	3	4	⑤
Becomes disoriented after bending over sink or table	1	②	3	4	5
Turns whole body to look at you	1	②	3	4	5
Touch					
Expresses discomfort at dental work or toothbrushing	1	②	3	4	5
Reacts emotionally or aggressively to touch	1	②	3	4	5
Rubs or scratches out a spot that has been touched	1	2	③	4	5
Gags easily with food textures, feeding utensils in mouth	1	2	③	4	5
Doesn't seem to notice when someone touches arm or back	1	②	3	4	5
Body Position					
Frequently changes body position	①	2	3	4	5
Locks joints (e.g., elbows, knees) for stability	1	②	3	4	5
Walks on toes	1	2	3	④	5
Moves stiffly	①	2	3	4	5
Has a weak grasp *Tim has a very tight grasp!*	1	2	3	4	⑤
Seems to have weak muscles	①	2	3	4	5
Emotional\Social					
Needs more protection from life than other children	1	2	③	4	5
Has trouble "growing up"	1	②	3	4	5
Doesn't have a sense of humor	1	②	3	④	5
Has difficulty making friends	1	②	3	4	5

Figure 5.12 Sensory Profile

Adapted from *Performance of typical children on the Sensory Profile: An item analysis* by Dunn, W. Copyright © 1994 by the American Occupational Therapy Association, Inc. Reprinted with permission.

Date: *October 13*

Student's Information:

Name: *Tim*

Number of students in class: *32*   **Number of student assistants:** *0*

Will this student require specially designed instruction in order to learn? *Absolutely*

Describe this students strengths and weaknesses. Rank them in order of their importance.

(5 = most important; 1 = least important)

Strengths	Rank	Weaknesses	Rank
Knows all of the students' names	*2*	*Doesn't complete assignments*	*5*
Interested in many things	*3*	*Has difficulty following directions*	*1*
Enjoys books	*1*	*Too active and clumsy*	*3*
		Disruptive outbursts	*4*
		Unable to print	*2*

Please check the appropriate box:

	Printing	Reading	Concepts
Above average			
Average		✔	
Below average	✔		✔

Figure 5.13 Teacher Questionnaire

School Performance Profile (Page 2)

Does this student exhibit any of the following problems in class?	Yes	No
Independence at school		
Leaves clothing twisted on body	✔	
Has difficulty with buttons, zippers, laces, or fasteners	✔	
Requires assistance to toilet self at school		✔
Class participation in projects		
Doesn't seem to notice when face or hands are messy	✔	
Has difficulty with cutting	✔	
Has difficulty with paper-pencil work	✔	
Has difficulty following through on instructions from others	✔	
Participation in physical education and recess		
Becomes overly excited after a movement activity	✔	
Appears lethargic		✔
Seems to have weak muscles		✔
Can't lift heavy objects		✔
Academic preparation		
Has difficulty putting puzzles together	✔	
Uses inefficient ways of doing things	✔	
Doesn't perceive body language or facial expressions	✔	
Overly serious	✔	
Poor attention span	✔	
Group work and social skills		
Doesn't respond when name is called	✔	
Avoids eye contact	✔	
Has difficulty standing in line or close to other people	✔	
Is overly affectionate with others		✔
Has temper tantrums	✔	
Hyperactive; distractible	✔	
Often does not seem to listen to what is being said to him or her	✔	

Figure 5.14 School Performance Profile

Adapted from *Performance of typical children on the Sensory Profile: An item analysis* by Dunn, W. Copyright
© 1994 by the American Occupational Therapy Association, Inc. Reprinted with permission.

COMPS Scoring Sheet

Name ___Tim___

Test Date _____ Date of Birth _____ Age _6yr3 7mon_ Sex _m_

Grade ___1___ School _Green Valley Elementary School_

1. Slow Movements

	Outward	Inward	
Symmetry	2	2	– symmetrical
	(1)	(1)	– some asymmetry
	0	0	– completely asymmetrical
Quality of Performance	2	2	– smooth
	(1)	(1)	– some irregularity
	0	0	– jerky
Speed	2	2	– 5 or more seconds
	(1)	(1)	– 3 to 4 seconds
	0	0	– 0 to 2 seconds

Total: ___6___ /12

Comments: _Wanted to do task before administrator was finished_

2. Rapid Forearm Rotation

Number of rotations   R   _12_

Number of rotations   L   _13_

Number of rotations   Both   _7_

R	L	Both	
(4)	(4)	4	9 or more rotations in 10 seconds
3	3	(3)	4-8 rotations in 10 seconds
2	2	2	1-3 rotations in 10 seconds
1	1	1	Unable to complete task

Total: ___11___ /12

Comments: _Had to be instructed to sit up._

Figure 5.15 COMPS Scoring Sheet

COMPS Scoring Sheet (page 2)

3. Finger-Nose Touching

	3	2	1	0	Eyes Open: RIGHT moving	Eyes Closed: RIGHT moving	Eyes Open: LEFT moving	Eyes Closed: LEFT moving
Movement of moving arm	Smooth, direct	Irregular or weaving movements	Confused jerky movements	Unable to sustain finger-nose pattern	2	2	2	2
Extended arm	Completely extended	30° or less of elbow flexion	More than 30° of elbow flexion		1	1	2	2
Force of touch of nose or finger	Lightly touching finger and nose	Minimal pushing (2 or fewer times)	Pushing 3 or more times		2	2	2	2
Missed contact	0 or 1 miss of nose or finger	2 or more misses of nose or finger	2 or more misses of both finger and nose		1	1	1	2

Lowest score for each trial: _1_ + _1_ + _1_ + _2_

= Total: _5_ /12

Comments: _____

4. Prone Extension

Duration

3 — 30 seconds or more   2 — 20-29 seconds   1 — 6-19 seconds   (0) — 0-5 seconds

Quality

a. Assumes

2 — All body parts simultaneously

(1) — Segmentally

0 — Cannot assume

c. Upper Trunk

2 — Definite arch, elbows and shoulders even

(1) — Minimal arch, elbows forward, or varies

0 — Chest on mat

b. Head

(2) — Face raised forward; neck extended > 45°

1 — Face looking at mat or slightly forward; neck extended < 45°, or varies

0 — Head on mat

d. Thighs

2 — Clearly off midthigh distally

1 — Barely off mat, or intermittent extension

(0) — Thighs on mat

COMPS Scoring Sheet (page 3)

e. Knees

2 — Flexion < 45°

1 — Flexion 46°-90°

(0) — Flexion > 90°

f. Maintains *(based on first 15 seconds)*

2 — Maintains and counts

1 — Maintains but body sways, limbs move, grimaces or does not count, or holds breath

(0) — Not assumed or maintained

Total: _4_/12   10-12 points = 3   7-9 points = 2   3-6 points = 1   0-2 points = 0

(Quality)   Quality Score: _/_/3

5. ATNR

3 — Elbow flexion from 0° to 30°, including visible muscle tone changes.

2 — Elbow flexion 31° to 60°, with slight depression of the shoulder.

1 — Elbow flexion more than 60°, but no loss of balance or lifting of contralateral leg. Shoulder is depressed and movement of the trunk will occur.

0 — Elbow flexed more than 60° with loss of the quadrupedal position due to collapse, forearm touching the surface, or contralateral leg leaving surface.

0 — Score 0 if child locks elbows in spite of verbal and physical prompts not to.

	Left Arm Scores (head to right)	*Right Arm Scores* (head to left)
1 — R _2_	1. _2_	2. _1_
2 — L _1_	4. _2_	3. _2_
3 — L _2_	5. _2_	6. _2_
4 — R _2_	8. _2_	7. _1_
5 — R _2_		
6 — L _2_		
7 — L _1_		
8 — R _2_	Total R: _8_	Total L: _6_
		Total R + L: _14_ /24

Comments: _____

6. Supine Flexion

Duration

3 — 30 seconds or more   2 — 20-29 seconds   (1) — 6-19 seconds   0 — 0-5 seconds

Quality

a. Assumes

(2) — All body parts simultaneously

1 — Segmentally

0 — Cannot assume

b. Neck

2 — Chin tucked, neck flexion > 45°

1 — Chin protrudes, neck flexion < 45°; or varies

(0) — Head not raised

COMPS Scoring Sheet (page 4)

c. Upper Trunk

   2 — Definite trunk flexion

   (1)— Trunk in neutral or extended position, or varies

   0 — Back on floor

e. Knees

   2 — Flexion > 90°

   (1)— Flexed 45°-90°, or varies

   0 — Flexion < 45°

d. Hips

   2 — Flexed > 90°

   (1)— Flexed 45°-90°, or varies

   0 — Flexed < 45°

f. Maintains *(based on first 15 seconds)*

   2 — maintains and counts

   1 — maintains but body sways, limbs move, grimaces, does not count, or holds breath

   (0)— Cannot assume or maintain

Total: _5_ /12   10-12 points = 3   7-9 points = 2   3-6 points = 1   0-2 points = 0

(Quality)   **Quality Score:** _1_ /3

Final Score

			Weighted Score (See tables 1-3)
1.	**Slow Motion**	_____	_____
2.	**Rapid Forearm Rotation**	_____	_____
3.	**Finger-Nose Touching**	_____	_____
4.	**Prone Extension**		
	_1_ + _____ = _____ x 2 = _____		_____
	Quality Duration		
5.	**ATNR**		
	_____ divided by 2 = _____		_____
6.	**Supine Flexion**		
	_1_ + _____ = _____ x 2 = _____		_____
	Quality Duration		

                                        Total   _____

                                        Minus adjustment
(see Tables 1-3)   _____

                                        Weighted Total Score _____

By the middle of October, Meredith had established a caseload measurement system to guide her treatment planning and document therapy needs within the school district (American Occupational Therapy Association 1989). Fifty-seven percent of school-based occupational therapists surveyed in 1994 indicated that they set their own caseloads and provide service to 22–40 students (Chandler 1994b). As Meredith had been very busy since September, she decided to review her caseload to determine the type and amount of service she could provide to Tim. By October, Meredith's caseload assignment of students requiring direct service was 15; consultation was 4; and monitoring was 2. Like most school-based therapists (85%), Meredith traveled to two or three schools a day (Chandler 1994a).

Meredith will be attending the IEP meeting next week. She is expected to contribute her impressions in the following areas:

- Whether Tim qualifies for OT
- His current level of performance
- Annual educational goals
- Short-term objectives
- Projected dates for initiation of therapy services
- Reevaluation criteria and schedule
- Anticipated duration of these services

(P.L. 101-476)

The Challenge

You are Meredith. Now that you have completed your screening, synthesize the information contained within this case to prepare for the IEP meeting and determine your course of action with Tim and Mr. L. If you would like assistance with this challenge, use the following questions and resources to aid your analysis. Complete questions 1, 2, 3, 6, 7, 9, and 12 at a minimum. See Selected Answers in Appendix E.

Questions to Aid Analysis

1. What are the self-care, productive work, and leisure play competencies of a 6-year 7-month-old boy?

2. Why do you think Meredith decided to use the COMPS? Score and interpret Tim's test results. See Appendix D for test score results. See Figures 5.15–5.17.

A. Transfer the total score for each item onto the first column of the Final Score section (on the last page of the score sheet). The quality of scores for Prone Extension and Supine Flexion will need to be transformed from 0-12 to 0-3 points before writing them:

> 10-12 points = 3
> 7-9 points = 2
> 3-6 points = 1
> 0-2 points = 0

B. For Prone Extension and Supine Flexion, add the *quality* and the *duration* scores, then multiply by *2*. For the Asymmetric Tonic Neck Reflex (ATNR) score, divide the total by *2*.

C. Locate the raw score on the left-hand side of Figure 5.17 and the item across the top to find the Weighted Score. Record this weighted score in the last column of the Final Score section.

D. Add the six Weighted Scores to obtain a total. Subtract the Adjustment for the age of the child (found at the bottom of Figure 5.17) from the Total, to obtain the Weighted Total Score.

E. A score *less than zero* indicates problems in Postural and Motor skills. Scores of *more than zero* are indicative of normal functioning in this area.

F. It is recommended that each score then be double-checked: the addition of each item, the transfer to the Final Score section, the conversion to a weighted score, the addition of all scores, and the subtraction of the adjustment. Therapists must remember that the clinical decisions they make regarding a child are at least partly based on test scores, and they are responsible for ensuring that these scores are accurate (Wilson et al. 1994, 19).

Figure 5.16 Scoring Instructions (COMPS)

Final weighted score for children aged 6 years 0 months to 7 years 11 months						
	Item					
Score	SM	RFR	FNT	PE	ATNR	SF
0	0	0	0	0	0	0
1	.22	.46	.03	-.04	-.07	.29
2	.44	.92	.06	-.08	-.14	.58
3	.66	1.38	.09	-.12	-.21	.87
4	.88	1.84	.12	-.16	-.28	1.16
5	1.10	2.30	.15	-.20	-.35	1.45
6	1.32	2.76	.18	-.24	-.42	1.74
7	1.54	3.22	.21	-.28	-.49	2.03
8	1.76	3.68	.24	-.32	-.56	2.32
9	1.98	4.14	.27	-.36	-.63	2.61
10	2.20	4.60	.30	-.40	-.70	2.90
11	2.42	5.06	.33	-.44	-.77	3.19
12	2.64	5.52	.36	-.48	-.84	3.48
Adjustment = 8.54						

Figure 5.17 Final Weighted Scores

Scoring instructions and final weighted scores adapted from Wilson et al. 1994. *Clinical Observations of Motor and Postural Skills.* Tucson, AZ: Therapy Skill Builders.

3. Complete the following chart by delineating Tim's occupational role performance, the performance components and contexts that impact them, and finally some behavioral observations supporting these claims. The *Uniform Terminology for Occupational Therapy* document from the American Occupational Therapy Association (1994) is a taxonomy system that will assist you in this process. By documenting behavioral evidence, you can more easily define measurable, behavioral, and objective outcome indicators. The chart has been started for you.

Occupational Performance Area Concerns (Self-Care, Productive Work and Leisure)	Contributory Performance Components and Contexts	Supporting Behavioral Observations
Activities of Daily Living		
Productive Work		
Leisure Play		
Unsafe on the playground	*Poor attention span* *Impulsive* *Poor balance*	*Average activity attention span during recess is 3 to 4 minutes. Does not wait his turn for equipment. Uses playground apparatus inappropriately. Unable to stand on one foot and avoids balance challenges. Frequently trips.*

4. Do you believe that Tim has a learning disability? According to what definition?

5. Do you think that Tim meets any of the diagnostic criteria within the *Diagnostic and Statistical Manual (4th Edition) (DSM-IV)* (American Psychiatric Association 1994)? If so, what will you do? How will this diagnosis affect his eligibility for OT as a related service under IDEA (See House Report 101–544, 1728; P.L. 101–476, Sec. 102).

6. Is Tim eligible and appropriate for your services? In the United States, OT services provided under IDEA funding must meet the criteria of "children with disabilities" (P.L. 101–476 Sec. 101(a)(1); House Report 101–544 Sec. 602 (1)(A), 62).

7. Define your present impressions regarding OT's potential to assist this child in terms of developing skills, restoring function, maintaining ability, and preventing dysfunction (Canadian Association of Occupational Therapists 1990). You will have the opportunity to update and refine these impressions at a later date, should you decide to pursue a full evaluation. Is Tim a candidate for a full evaluation?

8. Evaluate how much time you require to provide direct services to the clients on your current caseload. Use the AOTA (1989) document to assist you.

9. Plan your strategy for the IEP meeting. Give consideration to the people involved and to the questions that may arise. Be prepared to articulate your professional impressions, judgments, and recommendations. Mr. L. will be expecting specific feedback and recommendations. What will you tell him?

10. What do you think about Mr. L.'s comment, "Tim needs a special class and a teacher who has more experience at this sort of thing"? Does Tim have legal rights to inclusion? How does the law define *least restrictive environment*? (P.L. 101–476; see Appendix B.)

11. If you decide to pursue a full evaluation, how will this be performed (in or outside of class, during or after school)?

12. Assume that you have decided to provide service, what form will this take (direct, consultation, monitoring)? Assume that you have decided to complete an evaluation. What standardized test(s) would you consider administering? Refer to Appendix A for assistance.

New Terminology

children with disabilities
COMPS
consultation
DSM-IV
Education for All Handicapped Children Act

Individual Education Plan (IEP)
Individuals with Disabilities Education Act (IDEA)
least restrictive environment

learning disabled (LD)
monitoring
P.L. 94–142
P.L. 101–476
related service

Learning Resources

Information on the COMPS is available in Appendix A. Information on accessing Public Law and House Reports is available in Appendix B. Canadian readers should use the uniform terminology proposed in the Client-Centred Model of Occupational Performance outlined in Appendix C.

American Occupational Therapy Association. 1989. *Guidelines for occupational therapy services in school systems.* Bethesda, MD: American Occupational Therapy Association.

American Occupational Therapy Association. 1991. Statement: Occupational therapy provision for children with learning disabilities and/or mild to moderate perceptual and motor deficits. *American Journal of Occupational Therapy* 45:1069–73.

American Occupational Therapy Association. 1994. Uniform terminology for occupational therapy–3d ed. *American Journal of Occupational Therapy* 48:1047–54.

Canadian Association of Occupational Therapists. 1990. *Position paper on occupational therapy in schools.* Toronto: Canadian Association of Occupational Therapists.

Dunn, W. 1988. Models of occupational therapy service in the school system. *American Journal of Occupational Therapy* 42:718–23.

Dunn, W. 1994. Performance of typical children on the sensory profile: An item analysis. *American Journal of Occupational Therapy* 48:967–73.

Jones, C. B. 1991. *Sourcebook for children with attention deficit disorder.* Tucson, AZ: Therapy Skill Builders.

Missiuna, C., and H. Polatajko. 1995. Developmental dyspraxia by any other name: Are they all just clumsy children? *American Journal of Occupational Therapy* 49:619–27.

Polatajko, H., A. M. Fox, and C. Missiuna. 1995. An international consensus on children with developmental coordination disorder. *Canadian Journal of Occupational Therapy* 62:3–6.

U.S. House of Representatives. 1975. *Education of the Handicapped.* Public Law 94-142. Washington, D.C.

U.S. House of Representatives. 1990. *Education of the Handicapped Act Amendments of 1990.* House Report 101-544. Washington, D.C.

U.S. House of Representatives. 1990. *Individuals with Disabilities Education Act.* Public Law 101–476. Washington, D.C.

Wilson, B., N. Pollock, B. J. Kaplan, M. Law, and P. Faris. 1992. Reliability and construct validity of the *clinical observations of motor and postural skills.* *American Journal of Occupational Therapy* 46:775–83.

References

American Occupational Therapy Association. 1989. *Guidelines for occupational therapy services in school systems.* Rockville, MD: American Occupational Therapy Association.

American Occupational Therapy Association. 1991. 1990 Membership data survey. *OT Week* 5:1–8.

American Psychiatric Association. 1994. *Diagnostic and Statistical Manual-4th ed.* Washington, D.C.: American Psychiatric Association.

Chandler, B. E. 1994a. Who works in the schools? *OT Week* 8:24.

Chandler, B. E. 1994b. Keeping occupied at school. *OT Week* 8:24.

Cook, D. 1991. The Assessment Process. In *Pediatric occupational therapy: facilitating effective service provision,* edited by Dunn, W. Thorofare, NJ: Slack.

Dunn, W., editor. 1991. *Pediatric occupational therapy: Facilitating effective service provision.* Thorofare, NJ: Slack.

Dunn, W. 1994. Performance of typical children on the sensory profile: An item analysis. *American Journal of Occupational Therapy* 48:967–74.

Royeen, C. B. 1987. TIP–Touch Inventory for Preschoolers: A pilot study. *Physical and Occupational Therapy in Pediatrics* 7:29–40.

Royeen, C. B., and J. C. Fortune. 1990. TIE—Touch Inventory for Elementary School Aged Children. *American Journal of Occupational Therapy* 44:155–59.

U.S. House of Representatives. 1986. *Education of All Handicapped Children Act.* Public Law 94–142. Washington, D.C.

U.S. House of Representatives. 1990. *Individuals with Disabilities Education Act.* Public Law 101–476. Washington, D.C.

Wilson, B. N. Pollock, B. J. Kaplan, and M. Law. 1994. *Clinical observations of motor and postural skills.* Tucson, AZ: Therapy Skill Builders.

Tim (Part II)

Meredith sat at her desk and reflected on her recent visit with Tim. She had completed his initial screening just over 2 months ago but was unable to see Tim for a complete evaluation due to her full caseload. Two weeks ago, she started his occupational therapy (OT) assessment.

Meredith had been trained to administer and interpret the *Sensory Integration and Praxis Tests* (SIPT) (Ayres 1989). After testing Tim, Meredith sent the raw scores away for computer scoring with Western Psychological Services. The ChromaGraph™ summary matched Tim's performance profile with Generalized Sensory Integration Dysfunction, which is one of six potential patterns that may emerge from SIPT standardization (Ayres 1989).

The Challenge

You are Meredith. Given this new diagnostic information and the data you collected in the previous case, determine your treatment and intervention plan with this child. If you would like assistance with this challenge, use the following questions and resources to aid your analysis.

Questions to Aid Analysis

1. Describe the sensory integration frame of reference theoretical constructs, assumptions, and postulates. How does A. Jean Ayres (1979) conceptualize the senses, the integration of their inputs, and their end products? How do Fisher et al. (1991) conceptualize the importance and contribution of sensory integration to adaptive functioning?

2. Describe the six patterns that emerge from SIPT standardization. If Tim's ChromaGraph™ profile were closely aligned to the Generalized Sensory Integration Dysfunction pattern, which of the 17 SIPT tests would he have found most difficult? Least difficult? Identify the clinical observations and behaviors you have observed in Tim that support or provide functional evidence of this profile.

3. Use the information you have compiled to identify Tim's occupational performance problems and to formulate goals and objectives that you feel an OT should address. Be prepared to discuss and modify these recommendations after discussing them with Tim, his parents, and teacher. Use the following outline.

Problem # 1:

Goal # 1:

Objective 1a:

Objective 1b:

Objective 1c:

Problem # 2:

Goal # 2:

Objective 2a:

Objective 2b:

Objective 2c:

Problem # 3:

Goal # 3:

Objective 3a:

Objective 3b:

Objective 3c:

Problem # 4:

Goal # 4:

Objective 4a:

Objective 4b:

Objective 4c:

Problem # 5:

Goal # 5:

Objective 5a:

Objective 5b:

Objective 5c:

4. Therapists who work with children with learning difficulties typically use a remedial and/or a functional approach to OT intervention. The remedial approach focuses on enhancing performance components within the individual. The functional approach promotes occupational behavior through training, practice, and the modification or adaptation of performance context. Do your recommendations follow a remedial or functional approach to OT intervention?

5. Using the following form, create four 30-minute treatment sessions to address your goals from a remedial perspective. Try to focus your initial treatment on foundation skills, as attainment here will reduce other symptomatology. Describe how your activities address the senses and their integration by facilitating adaptive responses.

How will you grade the activity to ensure that Tim is presented with an achievable challenge?

Treatment Activity used to Facilitate an Adaptive Response	Activity Components (intersensory integration)	Grading Opportunities to Balance Achievement with Challenge

6. What recommendations or activities will you provide that reflect a functional approach to OT intervention with Tim?

New Terminology

adaptive response
ChromaGraph™
dyspraxia on verbal command
generalized sensory integrative
  dysfunction
high average sensory integration
  and praxis

low average bilateral integration
  and sequencing
low average sensory integration
  and praxis
SIPT
visuo- and somatodyspraxia
Western Psychological Services

Learning Resources

Information on the *Sensory Integration and Praxis Tests* (SIPT) is available in Appendix A.

Ayres, A. J. 1979. *Sensory integration and the child.* Los Angeles: Western Psychological Services.

Fisher, A. G., E. A. Murray, and A. C. Bundy. 1991. *Sensory integration theory and practice.* Philadelphia: F. A. Davis.

Jones, C. B. 1991. *Sourcebook for children with attention deficit disorder: A management guide for early childhood professionals and parents.* Tucson, AZ: Communication Skill Builders.

Kramer, P., and J. Hinojosa. 1993. *Frames of reference for occupational therapy.* Baltimore: Williams & Wilkins.

Warger, C. L., and L. J. Heflin. 1994. *Managing behaviors: A therapist's guide.* Tucson, AZ: Communication Skill Builders.

Sensory integration therapeutic equipment is available from the following vendors:

Flaghouse
150 N. MacQuesten Parkway
Mt. Vernon, NY 10550
1-800-793-7900

Southpaw
P.O. Box 1047
Dayton, OH 45401-1047
1-800-228-1698

References

Ayres, A. J. 1989. *Sensory integration and praxis tests.* Baltimore: Williams & Wilkins.

Kramer, P., and J. Hinojosa. 1993. *Frames of reference for occupational therapy.* Baltimore: Williams & Wilkins.

Robert

The inner workings of the human mind are far more intricate
than the most complicated systems of modern technology. *

—Anderson 1995

Background

ABC Emergency Service was busy on July 28th. An 8-year-old trauma patient had just been admitted. Robert had been struck by a car while riding his bike. Although bicycle helmets reduce the risk of brain injury by 88% (Thompson et al. 1989), this child was not wearing his. The emergency room physician ordered immediate surgery. The diagnoses included parietal skull fracture, epidural hematoma with loss of consciousness, bifrontal contusions, fractured right tibia, and multiple head, trunk, and upper-limb abrasions.

Traumatic brain injury (TBI) is the most common cause of traumatic death and acquired disability in children and young adults (Ghajar and Hariri 1992; Michaud et al. 1993a). The overall risk of TBI in children is estimated at 4% in boys and 2.5% in girls (Rivara and Mueller 1986). Damage results from impact or inertial forces. Secondary damage may occur from hypoxia, hypotension, hemorrhage, cerebral edema, infection, and pressure necrosis. Recent studies of minor TBI suggest that neurotransmitter factors (cholinergic systems) may contribute to pathology (Katz and DeLuca 1992). Damage may occur where the blow is sustained (coup lesion), or to the brain tissue that impacts against the opposite inside of the skull (contrecoup). TBI is typically classified as either *closed* or *open*. The major causes of pediatric TBI are falls (42%), motor vehicle accidents (34%), and other circumstances (24%) (Molnar and Perrin 1992).

The sequelae of head trauma is broad and ranges from mild (82%), moderate or severe (14%), to fatal (5%) (Kraus et al. 1990). The effect of age on neurological outcome is complex, but children generally fare better than adults. Outcomes from TBI at very young ages are worse. According to Michaud et al. (1993a), cerebral water and neurochemical content, the extent of neural myelination, the stage of brain development, and localization of cortical function vary in children of different ages and impact on brain plasticity. Deficits include motor, communication, cognitive, sensory, behavioral, emotional, and integrative dysfunction; causing loss of independence in self-care, productive work, and leisure play occupational performance areas. These changes can have profound effects on a child's interpersonal relationships, role performance, and the emotional well-being of caregivers.

---

*Anderson, J. R. 1995. From *Cognitive Psychology and its Implications*. Copyright © by W. H. Freeman and Company. Reprinted with permission.

Robert, like the majority of TBI patients, experienced a period of unconsciousness. Unlike the dramatic awakenings depicted in novels, on television, and on the big screen, coma patients recover very gradually, and their progress may plateau at any stage of recovery (Fike et al. 1993). Cognitive dysfunction is the most likely outcome following TBI. Multidisciplinary team members frequently use the *Glasgow Coma Scale* (GCS) (Teasdale and Jennett 1974) and Rancho Los Amigos Hospital *Levels of Cognitive Functioning* (Hagen et al. 1979) to evaluate and document changes in level of arousal and cognition.

The GCS is a quick, simple, criterion-based behavioral scale used on initial admission to estimate injury severity. Motor, verbal, and eye-opening responses are evaluated. Because the GCS requires patients to speak, a Children's Coma Scale was developed for infants and toddlers. The maximum score on this scale is 11 (Ghajar and Hariri 1992). Robert was old enough, however, to be evaluated with the GCS.

By late August, the Pediatric Brain Injury Team at ABC Rehabilitation Center was notified that Robert had been transferred to their program from acute care. Debbie, the team occupational therapist, received the occupational therapy (OT) referral and began to review the medical chart. Robert's medical file indicated that he was unconscious at the scene, with pupils dilated and nonreactive. His GCS on admission after resuscitation was 5. GCS at 72 hours was 10. Robert's right leg cast was scheduled for removal in late September. Debbie spent her first week with Robert completing his initial rehabilitation OT evaluation.

The Occupational Therapy Evaluation Report that follows includes descriptions, notations, and personal observations that closely resemble the format a clinician might use to complete a rehabilitation OT evaluation.

Occupational Therapy Evaluation Report

I. Introduction
This 8-year 1-month-old boy was diagnosed with TBI and right tibia fracture, following a bicycling accident on July 28 when he was hit by a car. Admitted to ABC Rehabilitation Center inpatient Pediatric Brain Injury Program on August 28 (from ABC Emergency Service) and seen for OT rehabilitation evaluation between August 29 and September 2. No significant previous medical history. See medical records for details of current illness. Using seizure medication. No allergies.

II. Assessment
Information contained in this report was collected from an interview with Robert's mother and the rehabilitation team (August 29), clinical observations, and standardized testing. All quotations below are from Robert's mother.

A. Occupational Performance Areas–Daily Living Skills
Self-Care (Premorbid) Robert had age-appropriate skills in all areas of personal self-care prior to his accident. He dressed himself independently and fashionably each morning and was responsible for keeping his room clean. He was able to make breakfast and sandwich

---

lunches for himself. Occasionally, he made soup for the family. He learned to bake in early childhood and could prepare cookies with minimal supervision. Robert opened a bank account 6 months ago to "deposit all the money he made selling lemonade and popcorn at the baseball games."

Now, Robert requires moderate assistance (Robert performs 50–75% of the task) with dressing. He has difficulty organizing and orienting clothing articles, which is very frustrating for him. He requires maximum assistance (Robert performs 25–50% of the task) to manage small clothing fasteners, lace his shoes, or tie his shoelaces. Hygiene activities require close supervision, as Robert has difficulty labeling and determining the use of common objects. For example, Robert attempted to place tube hand lotion, rather than toothpaste, on his toothbrush. Robert has difficulty moving his toothbrush with any speed and does not completely and thoroughly brush his teeth. However, he is able to wash his hands and face independently, once set up.

At mealtimes, Robert brings food to his mouth and swallows without difficulty. Video fluoroscopy studies were performed in early August, with normal results. Mealtime supervision is required, as Robert throws food (average = two times/meal), spills his drink (average = one time/meal), and refuses to use utensils (100% of the time). Robert is unable to open plastic containers, lids, and soda-can tabs but slowly screws and unscrews kitchen jars on his own. Robert's home management responsibilities include vacuuming, keeping his room "decent," occasionally washing dishes, and cooking.

Robert requires minimal assistance (Robert performs 75–100% of the task) transferring to a bed, the toilet, and the bathtub from the wheelchair (w/c). Robert walks short distances on his right lower extremity (L/E) walking cast with a therapist and a rolling walker. He loses his balance every 3–4 minutes. The Pediatric Brain Injury Team and Robert's mother have decided to keep him in a w/c with a seat belt until his balance and judgment improve. Robert has attempted to walk alone without supervision on three occasions, despite safety risks. He becomes frustrated with his w/c when he has difficulty negotiating corners and small areas (e.g., bathroom).

Productive Activities Robert "excels in school and has many friends." He receives "A's and B+'s in all subjects but is especially talented in math and science. . . . He was slow at learning to read, but he is very persistent." The school liaison team consultant supports these claims. Refer to Robert's report card for details. Academic readiness testing will be completed with neuropsychology when appropriate.

Leisure Robert developed "socially and physically just like all the other kids" but was "exceptionally social, with so many friends." He "always liked to be the organizer." He "enjoys biking, rugby, video games, skateboarding, baseball, rugby, and computers." Robert is from a single-parent family and does not know his father. His one sister, Kathleen, is 4 years old. Mother has worked full-time as a waitress for years. The extended family all live "across the country," and mother "doesn't talk to them much." Robert has begun recreation therapy and attends evening groups.

B. Performance Components and Contexts that Affect Daily Living
Sensory Awareness and Processing Localization of upper extremity (U/E) touch is within normal limits (WNL). No tactile defensiveness or sensitivities noted. Distinguishes hot and cold temperature. Identifies two of five common objects with his right U/E, and three of five with his left U/E with vision occluded. Positive Romberg's sign. Gross assessment of oculomotor control indicates that alignment is WNL, but incomplete visual scanning with jerky tracking. No gross deficits with hearing are noted. Scheduled for formal vision assessment.

Perceptual Processing Robert was screened with the *Motor-Free Visual Perceptual Test-Revised* (MVPT-R) (Colarusso and Hammill 1996).

When asked to draw a clock, Robert includes all numbers on the right side of a predrawn circle. He takes 3 minutes to complete this task, as he has to recount numbers from 1 on five occasions. Initially, he does not include the number 7, until verbally cued to ensure that he has not made any errors. Misses 60% of *E* letters on left side of scanning work sheet placed in midline (100% accurate on right side of work sheet). Robert has difficulty with three-dimensional construction. He completes a five-block house but not a five-block gate or six-block airplane or pyramid. He was able to build a 10-block (1″ wooden cubes) tower.

Neuromusculoskeletal Quality of movement is affected by mild generalized hypotonia with poor proximal cocontraction. Hyperreflexia at very end ranges of biceps and triceps. L/E not assessed with quick stretch. Full U/E active range of motion (ROM). No pain on passive or active ROM. See physical therapy report for detailed L/E ROM. All L/E joints outside of the cast appear within normal limits but not formally assessed. Today, Robert tolerates 3 hours of therapy per day but tires easily and takes a short morning and afternoon nap.

Motor Robert walks short distances with therapist supervision but frequently loses his balance. He is unable to stand on his left foot for longer than 1 or 2 seconds without losing his balance. Right dominant premorbidly. Positive U/E cerebellar signs on testing: ataxic reach, dysmetria, and dysdiadochokinesis. Able to hold scissors and slowly snip with jagged-cut lines but unable to cut a predrawn square or circle pattern or cut between two parallel lines (3″ apart). Although we have not yet completed the *Bruininks-Oseretsky Test of Motor Proficiency* (Bruininks 1978), Robert has great difficulty picking up and placing pennies and small pegs. Uses a static tripod pencil grip. Visual motor skills, as measured by the *Developmental Test of Visual Motor Integration* (VMI-R) (Beery 1989), are impaired. Robert's raw score is 12 and age equivalency is 6 years 3 months.

Cognitive Integration Poor short- and long-term memory, with the former more impaired than the latter. Disoriented to time and place. Raw score results on the *Children's Orientation and Amnesia Test* (Ewings-Cobbs et al. 1990) was 87/124. Distracted by extraneous noises and own ideas. Once distracted, Robert has difficulty redirecting himself or remembering the task instructions. Perseverates on conversation themes and questions and requires extra time to process questions before answering. Impulsive in responses. Task attention span 3–5 minutes before he becomes restless or frustrated. Threw one object in first 10 minutes of testing, and four objects within the last 10 minutes of a 30-minute evaluation session. Frequency of throwing objects increases with frustration.

Psychosocial Skills Emotionally labile, with occasional (2 to 3 times/day) verbal outbursts. No crying episodes. No apparent insight into current deficits. Not safety conscious when ambulating or when performing tasks at the sink. Robert is watchful of other patients but has not made new friends. During yesterday's lunch, Robert wanted to direct nursing staff concerning where all of the children should sit.

C. Parent-Identified Issues and Concerns
Mother indicates that she is concerned about Robert's behavior and "misconduct at meals." "He has always had such good eating habits. . . . He's just not the same person. . . . He seems so different, . . . He certainly doesn't seem to remember very much from day to day." "Naturally, I'm happy that he wasn't more seriously hurt, but I have high hopes for him. That's important; I think." Mother also expresses her concern about Robert's future educational potential.

III. Interpretation
Robert is an 8-year 1-month-old boy with TBI and a fractured right tibia, who was assessed upon transfer to the Pediatric Brain Injury Program just over 1 month post injury. To date, he has attained a Rancho Los Amigos Level V. He continues to require moderate to maximal assistance in most areas of daily living, although some basic activities can be performed with close supervision and cueing. Robert's global dependence in self-care, educational, and leisure pursuits is secondary to impairments in sensory, perceptual, neuromusculoskeletal, cognitive, and psychosocial abilities. His behavior remains socially inappropriate and unsafe due to impaired insight, memory, judgment, and impulsiveness. These features also limit Robert's ability to be safe on his own during self-care and to analyze or anticipate the consequences of his actions. Robert's family continues to grieve for Robert and their losses and to verbalize limited understanding about his current behavior.

The Challenge

Debbie must identify and define specific functional problems that currently limit Robert's ability to succeed in daily activity challenges within the hospital, home, and community. Throughout the treatment process, Debbie will pay particular attention to issues of importance to Robert and his family. Robert's expected length of stay at ABC Rehabilitation Center is 1 month.

You are Debbie. Now that you have completed your evaluation (a) identify functional problems that limit Robert's ability to succeed in daily living challenges; (b) establish short- and long-term goals and objectives; and (c) design your intervention plan. If you would like assistance with this challenge, use the questions and resources below to aid your analysis. Complete questions 1, 3, 5-13 at a minimum. See Selected Answers in Appendix E.

Questions to Aid Analysis

1. What are the activities, roles, and tasks of an 8-year-old child? Can you classify these abilities into occupational performance areas—self-care, productive work, and leisure play?

2. Describe Robert's volitional (personal causation, interests, and values), habituation (habits, patterns, and roles), and performance skill subsystems. How do these competencies and occupational roles differ from his premorbid self?

3. How does Robert's current occupational role performance compare to the norm?

The observational and testing information contained within this case has been designed to provide you with the opportunity to become familiar with various assessment tools. Formal training, practice apprenticeship, and qualified peer reviews, however, are required for test administration competency.

What do you think of Robert's performance on the COAT test? (See Figure 5.18.) Refer to Figure 5.19 for normative data.

What do you think of Robert's performance on the MVPT-R? Score and interpret this assessment. See Figure 5.20.

See Appendix D for test score results.

CHILDREN'S ORIENTATION AND AMNESIA TEST (COAT)

General Orientation:

1. What is your name? first (2) _Rob_
   last (3) _Smith_   (5)   **5**

2. How old are you? (3) _"7"_ When is your birthday?
   month (1) ✓ day (1) ✓   (5)   **2**

3. Where do you live? city (3) ✓
   state (2) ✓   (5)   **5**

4. What is your father's name? (5) ____
   What is your mother's name? (5) ✓   (10)   **10**

5. What school do you go to? (3) ✓
   What grade are you in? (2) _"one"_   (5)   **3**

6. Where are you now? (5) _"hospital"_   (5)   **5**
   (May rephrase question: Are you at home now? Are
   you in the hospital? If rephrased, child must correctly
   answer both questions to receive credit.)

7. Is it daytime or night-time? (5) ____   (5)   **5**

            General Orientation Total   **35**

Temporal Orientation (administer if age 8 -15)

8. What time is it now (5) ____   (5)   **2**
   (correct = 5; < hr. off = 4; 1 hr. off = 3; (>1 hr. off = 2;)
   2 hrs. off = 1)

9. What day of the week is it? (5) ____   (5)   **3**
   (correct = 5; 1 off = 4; (2 off = 3;) 3 off = 2; 4 off = 1)

10. What day of the month is it? (5) ____   (5)   **3**
    (correct = 5; 1 off = 4; (2 off = 3;) 3 off = 2; 4 off = 1)

11. What is the month? (10) ____   (10)   **7**
    (correct = 10; (1 off = 7;) 2 off = 4; 3 off = 1)

12. What is the year? (15) ____   (15)   **10**
    (correct = 15; (1 off = 10;) 2 off = 5; 3 off = 1)

            Temporal Orientation Total   **25**

Memory:

13. Say these numbers after me in the same order. (Discontinue
    when the child fails both series of digits at any length. Score
    2 points if both digit series are correctly repeated; score 1 point
    if only 1 is correct.)

			X	X	
(3)	(5) 2		35296	81493 Ø	
(58)	(42) 2		539418	724856 ___	
(643)	(926) 2		8129365	4739128 ___	(14) **7**
(7216)	3279 1				
	X				

14. How many fingers am I holding up? Two fingers (2) ✓
    Three fingers (3) ✓ Ten fingers (5) ✓   (10)   **10**

15. Who is on Sesame Street? (10) ✓
    (can substitute other major television show)   (10)   **10**

16. What is my name? (10) ____ ?   (10)   **Ø**

            Memory Total   **27**

            OVERALL TOTAL   **87**

Figure 5.18 *Children's Orientation and Amnesia Test* (COAT)

Reprinted with permission. Ewings-Cobbs, L., H. S. Levin, J. M. Fletcher, M. E. Miner, and H. M. Eisenbery. 1990. Children's orientation and amnesia test: Relationship to severity of acute head injury and to recovery of memory. *Neurosurgery* 27(5):683–91.

Age (year)	n	Total Score * Mean	Standard Deviation
3	16	46.8	12.6
4	26	59.4	8.5
5	25	61.6	6.3
6	12	64.1	8.5
7	10	68.3	6.1
8	17	114.8	5.6
9	8	113.3	7.4
10	14	117.6	5.7
11	10	116.4	4.1
12–15	8	119.8	1.5

* For ages 3 to 7 years the total score is based on the general orientation (Questions 1–7) and memory (Questions 13–16) items. The total score for children aged 8 to 15 years is based on Questions 1 to 16.

Figure 5.19 Normative Data for the *Children's Orientation and Amnesia Test* (COAT)

Reprinted with permission. Ewings-Cobbs, L., H. S. Levin, J. M. Fletcher, M. E. Miner, and H. M. Eisenbery. 1990. Children's orientation and amnesia test: Relationship to severity of acute head injury and to recovery of memory. *Neurosurgery* 27(5):683–91.

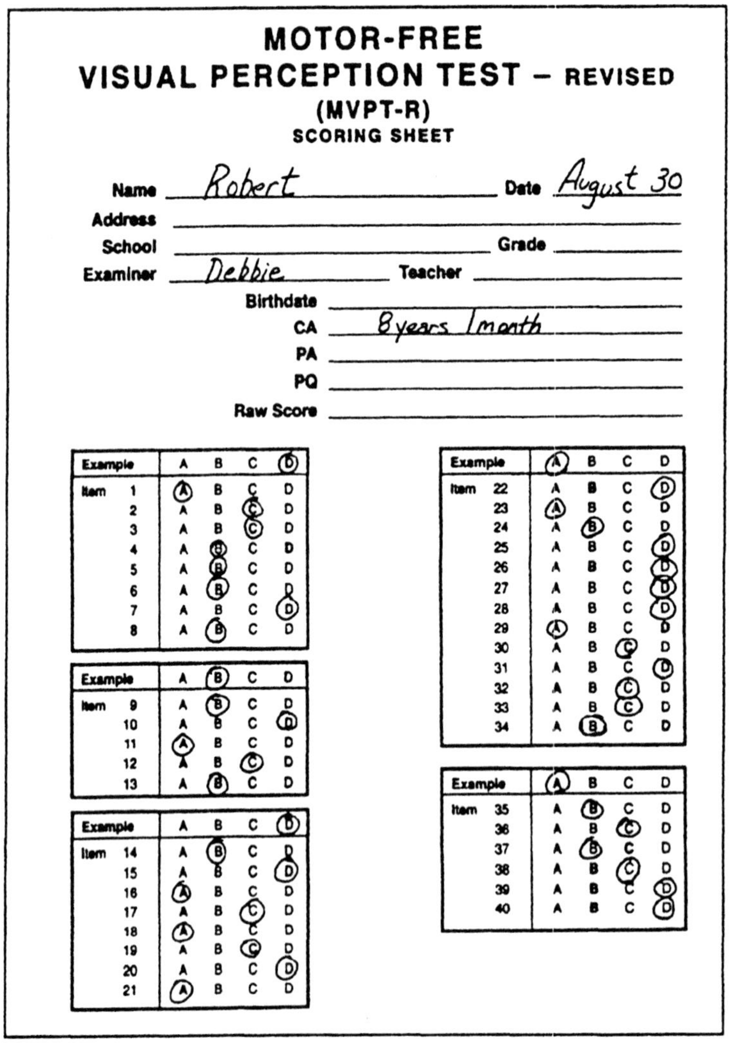
MOTOR-FREE
VISUAL PERCEPTION TEST – REVISED
(MVPT-R)
SCORING SHEET

Name Robert Date August 30
Address
School Grade
Examiner Debbie Teacher
Birthdate
CA 8 years 1 month
PA
PQ
Raw Score

Example	A	B	C	D
Item 1	A	B	C	D
2	A	B	C	D
3	A	B	C	D
4	A	B	C	D
5	A	B	C	D
6	A	B	C	D
7	A	B	C	D
8	A	B	C	D

Example	A	B	C	D
Item 9	A	B	C	D
10	A	B	C	D
11	A	B	C	D
12	A	B	C	D
13	A	B	C	D

Example	A	B	C	D
Item 14	A	B	C	D
15	A	B	C	D
16	A	B	C	D
17	A	B	C	D
18	A	B	C	D
19	A	B	C	D
20	A	B	C	D
21	A	B	C	D

Example	A	B	C	D
Item 22	A	B	C	D
23	A	B	C	D
24	A	B	C	D
25	A	B	C	D
26	A	B	C	D
27	A	B	C	D
28	A	B	C	D
29	A	B	C	D
30	A	B	C	D
31	A	B	C	D
32	A	B	C	D
33	A	B	C	D
34	A	B	C	D

Example	A	B	C	D
Item 35	A	B	C	D
36	A	B	C	D
37	A	B	C	D
38	A	B	C	D
39	A	B	C	D
40	A	B	C	D

Figure 5.20 *Motor-Free Visual Perception Test–Revised* Scoring Sheet

Reproduced with permission from Academic Therapy Publications.

Use the developmental information contained within the Peabody Developmental Motor Scales-Fine Motor Index *(Folio and Fewell 1983) and* Bruininks-Oseretsky Test of Motor Proficiency-Fine Motor Composite *(Bruininks 1978) to enhance your clinical judgments about Robert's fine motor and perceptual performance.*

Become familiar with the Pediatric Evaluation of Disability Inventory *(PEDI) (Haley et al. 1989), and the* Functional Independence Measure for children *(WeeFIM) (Granger and Hamilton 1992) to enrich your understanding of possible functional assessment tools used in pediatric rehabilitation services.*

4. What are your impressions of Robert's clock and person drawings? (Drawings are reduced in size.)

Figure 5.21 Robert's Clock and Person

5. Complete the chart on page 136 by delineating both this family's and your concerns regarding Robert's performance, the performance components and contexts that impact on them, and some behavioral observations supporting these claims. The *Uniform Terminology for Occupational Therapy* document from the American Occupational Therapy Association (1994) provides a taxonomy system that will assist you in this process. By documenting behavioral evidence, you can more easily define measurable and objective outcome indicators. The chart has been started for you.

6. What do you think of the issues identified by Robert's mother? Is there an assessment or interview instrument that would assist you in determining and prioritizing family issues and concerns? Refer to Appendix A and the article by M. E. Neistadt (1995) for assistance.

Occupational Performance Area Concerns (Self-Care, Productive Work, and Leisure)	Contributory Performance Components and Contexts	Supporting Behavioral Observations
1. Requires moderate to maximum assistance to dress self.	Poor attention, spatial relations, fine and gross motor dysfunction, and possible dyspraxia.	Maximal assistance with buttons and laces, difficulty organizing and orienting clothes. Can't determine use of common objects.
2.		
3.		
4.		
5.		

7. Given what you know about the personality and premorbid roles and skills of this 8-year-old patient, what are your goals as an occupational therapist? Ensure that your goals maintain or promote function and prevent dysfunction and that they fit the concerns, priorities, and resources of this family and Robert. Assume that Robert's mother has concurred with your recommendations. Write three short-term objectives for each goal using the following outline. Your objectives should be specific and measurable. Use Mahoney and Kannenberg (1992) for assistance.

Problem # 1: Robert requires moderate to maximum assistance to dress himself due to difficulties with attention, perception, and motoric abilities, and possible dyspraxia.

  Goal # 1: Robert will be able to dress himself in the morning with distant supervision.

      Objective 1a: Robert will organize his clothes in preparation for donning with one or two verbal cues within 5 minutes (September 10).

      Objective 1b: Robert will unbutton his shirt and tie his shoes with moderate assistance within 3 minutes per activity (September 10).

      Objective 1c:

Problem # 2:

  Goal # 2:

      Objective 2a:

      Objective 2b:

      Objective 2c:

Problem # 3:

  Goal # 3:

      Objective 3a:

      Objective 3b:

      Objective 3c:

Problem # 4:

   Goal # 4:

      Objective 4a:

      Objective 4b:

      Objective 4c:

Problem # 5:

   Goal # 5:

      Objective 5a:

      Objective 5b:

      Objective 5c:

8. How could you use the Model of Human Occupation to guide your evaluation and intervention planning?

9. How could you use the Visual-Perceptual frame of reference to guide your evaluation and intervention planning? Will you use a functional or remedial approach?

10. Could you use a Motor Control frame of reference to guide your evaluation and intervention planning?

11. Could you use a Sensory Integration frame of reference to guide your evaluation and intervention planning?

12. Using the form on page 139, create four 30-minute treatment sessions to address Robert's five performance goals and short-term objectives from question #7. Try to focus initial treatment on foundation or lower-level skills. Attainment here will reduce other symptomatology and reveal more specific dysfunction. In the first column, include a description of the theoretical model that led you to choose the activity.

13. Develop an intervention plan and strategies to address the needs of Robert's family. Can you incorporate these issues into the sessions you have developed from question #12?

14. Although your current evaluation and intervention plan is complete, a more thorough reevaluation of gross motor proficiency will eventually be required once Robert's cast is removed. What testing instrument would you use to determine Robert's gross motor competencies? Are there certain subtests you would omit on initial testing due to safety precautions? Use Appendix A for assistance in this area.

Activity Plan and Theoretical Model	Issue, Goal, and Objective Addressed	Grading Opportunities

15. After Robert is discharged, what special education and related services do you expect that he will receive from his school district? What classroom accommodations may be needed for Robert? How could you determine the type and extent of special education services provided in your area? Does Robert qualify for special education and related services according to the diagnostic groupings identified in the Individuals with Disabilities Education Act (Public Law 101–476, Section 101; House of Representatives Report 101–544 Section III)?

16. You have had the opportunity to be exposed to ABC Rehabilitation Center's OT evaluation documentation format and style. As a therapist involved in continuous quality improvement, determine which report-writing strategies you would like to incorporate into your work and identify areas where Debbie could improve.

New Terminology

ataxia
cerebellar signs
cholinergic systems
closed TBI
coup lesion
cocontraction
contrecoup lesion
dysmetria
dysdiadochokinesis
epidural hematoma

Glasgow Coma Scale
hyperreflexia
minimal/moderate/
  maximum assistance
MVPT-R
neuropsychology
open TBI
PEDI
perseveration

plasticity
praxis
premorbid
proprioception
Rancho Los Amigos Scale
resuscitation
static tripod pencil grip
video fluoroscopy
VMI-R

Learning Resources and Materials

Information on the MVPT-R, PEDI, PDMS, VMI-R and Wee Fim is available in Appendix A. Information on accessing Public Law and House Reports is available in Appendix B. Canadian readers should use the uniform terminology proposed in the Client-Centred Model of Occupational Performance (Canadian Association of Occupational Therapists 1983) outlined in Appendix C.

Abreu, B. C., and J. P. Toglia. 1987. Cognitive rehabilitation: A model for occupational therapy. *American Journal of Occupational Therapy* 41:439–48.

American Occupational Therapy Association. 1994. Uniform terminology for occupational therapy, 3d ed. *American Journal of Occupational Therapy* 48:1047–54.

Bell, T. A. 1994. Understanding students with traumatic brain injury: A guide for teachers and therapists. *School System Special Interest Section Newsletter of the AOTA* 1:1–4.

Boehm, R. 1988. *Improving upper body control: An approach to assessment and treatment of tonal dysfunction.* Tucson, AZ:Therapy Skill Builders.

Canadian Association of Occupational Therapists. 1983. *Guidelines for the Client-Centred Practice of Occupational Therapy*. Toronto: Canadian Association of Occupational Therapists.

Colarusso, R. P., and D. D. Hammill. 1996. *Motor-free visual perception test–revised*. Novato, CA: Academic Therapy Publications.

Ewing-Cobbs, L., H. S. Levin, J. M. Fletcher, M. E. Miner, and H. M. Eisenberg. 1990. The *children's orientation and amnesia test:* Relationship to severity of acute head injury to recovery of memory. *Neurosurgery* 27:683–91.

Haley, S. M., M. J. Baryza, J. E. Lewin, and M. I. Cioffi. 1991. Sensorimotor dysfunction in children with brain injury: Development of a data base for evaluation and research. *Physical and Occupational Therapy in Pediatrics* 11:1–26.

Kramer, P., and J. Hinojosa. 1993. *Frames of reference for pediatric occupational therapy*. Baltimore: Williams & Wilkins.

Mahoney, P., and K. Kannenberg. 1992. Writing functional goals. In *Effective documentation for occupational therapy*, edited by J. D. Acquaviva, 91–96. Rockville, MD: American Occupational Therapy Association.

Neistadt, M. E. 1995. Methods of assessing client's priorities: A survey of adult physical dysfunction settings. *American Journal of Occupational Therapy* 49:428–36.

Sellars, G. W., and C. H. Vegter. 1993. *Pediatric brain injury: A practical resource*. Tucson, AZ: Therapy Skill Builders.

Focus on Research

In 1990, 4.2% of occupational therapists and 3.9% of certified occupational therapy assistants in the United States indicated that TBI was the most frequent health problem in their clients (American Occupational Therapy Association 1991). Although the TBI literature predominantly focuses on adults, researchers have completed a number of studies on the motor and cognitive outcomes in TBI children. Ghajar and Harari (1992) suggest that 90% of the long-term neurological outcome has generally been achieved within 6 months to 1 year post-injury. Increases in intelligence quotients (IQ) scores continue throughout the first year after injury, with slow improvement thereafter (Molnar and Perrin 1992). GCS scores taken at 72 hours are better predictors of outcome than early scores (Michaud et al. 1993a).

When 14 TBI children, ages 5–15, with loss of consciousness for at least 24 hours, were compared to 14 children without TBI (matched for age and sex), highly significant differences were found in gross motor skills, 16 months post-injury, as measured by the *Bruininks-Oseretsky Test of Motor Proficiency* (Bruininks 1978). No significant differences were found on the Fine Motor Composite, but highly significant differences were found on the Upper-Limb Speed and Dexterity subtest (Chaplin et al. 1993).

When 40 children, age 1 month to 5.6 years, who had sustained mild to moderate TBI (with and without additional injuries), were compared to 17 children who had sustained non-central nervous system injuries, no significant differences were found in functional performance and family functioning 1 and 6 months after hospital discharge, as measured by the *Pediatric Evaluation of Disability Inventory* (PEDI), the *Child Behavior Checklist*, and the *Impact on Family Scale* (Coster et al. 1994).

When 98 children, age 6 to 15 years, with mild, moderate, and severe closed-head injuries were matched with individually selected controls, a pattern of decline in performance with increasing severity of TBI was seen in the areas of intelligence, memory, speeded motor performance, adaptive problem solving, and academic performance (Jaffe et al. 1992).

When 53 mild TBI children were compared to individually matched controls, no significant differences were found in long-term deficits in intellectual, neuropsychological, academic, or "real world" functioning, as measured by standardized and teacher questionnaires measuring social, educational, domestic, and community living skills (Fay et al. 1993). Michaud et al. (1993b) found a three-fold increased likelihood of a history of prior TBI among children in grades one through five who received special education services for behavioral disorders. This ratio increased to ninefold for children sustaining TBI in the preschool years. Full scale IQs for TBI children (*n*=170) was 88 (*sd*=5), compared to control group IQ of 107 (*sd*=14).

References

American Occupational Therapy Association. 1991. 1990 Membership Data Survey. *OT Week* 5:1–8.

Anderson, J. R. 1995. *Cognitive psychology and its implications*, 4th ed. New York: W. H. Freeman.

Bruininks, R. 1978. *Bruininks-Oseretsky test of motor proficiency*. Circle Pines, MN: American Guidance Service.

Chaplin, D., J. Deitz, and K. M. Jaffe. 1993. Motor performance in children after traumatic brain injury. *Archives of Physical Medicine and Rehabilitation* 74:161-64.

Colarusso, R. P., and D. D. Hammill. 1996. *Motor-free visual perception test–revised*. Novato, CA: Academic Therapy Publications.

Coster, W. J., S. Haley, and M. Baryza. 1994. Functional performance of young children after traumatic brain injury: A 6-month follow-up study. *American Journal of Occupational Therapy* 48:211–218.

Ewing-Cobbs, L., H. S. Levin, J. M. Fletcher, M. E. Miner, and H. M. Eisenberg. 1990. *Children's orientation and amnesia test*: Relationship to severity of acute head injury and to recovery of memory. *Neurosurgery* 27:683–91.

Fay, G. C., K. M. Jaffe, N. L. Polissar, S. Liao, K. M. Martin, H. A. Shurtleff, J. M. Rivara, and H. R. Winn. 1993. Mild pediatric traumatic brain injury: A cohort study. *Archives of Physical Medicine and Rehabilitation* 74:895–901.

Fike, M. L., M. Wiener, and S. Darlak. 1993. The young adult with a spinal injury. In *Practice issues in occupational therapy: Intraprofessional team building,* edited by S. E. Ryan, 93–102. Thorofare, NJ: Slack.

Ghajar, J., and R. J. Hariri. 1992. Management of pediatric head injury. *Pediatric Clinics of North America* 39:1093–1125.

Hagen, C., D. Malkmus, and P. Durham. 1979. *Levels of cognitive functioning.* Downey, CA: Rancho Los Amigos Hospital.

Jaffe, K. M., G. C. Fay, N. L. Polissar, K. M. Martin, H. Shurtleff, J. B. Rivara, and H. R. Winn. 1992. Severity of pediatric traumatic brain injury and early neurobehavioral outcome: A cohort study. *Archives of Physical Medicine and Rehabilitation* 73:540–47.

Katz, R. T., and J. DeLuca. 1992. Sequelae of minor traumatic brain injury. *American Family Physician* 46:1491–98.

Kraus, J. F., A. Rock, and P. Hemyari. 1990. Brain injuries among infants, children, adolescents and young adults. *American Journal of Diseases of Children* 144:684–91.

Michaud, L. J., A. Duhaime, and M. L. Batshaw. 1993a. Traumatic brain injury in children. *Pediatric Clinics of North America* 40:553–65.

Michaud, L. J., F. P. Rivara, K. M. Jaffe, G. Kay, and J. L. Dailey. 1993b. Traumatic brain injury as a risk factor for behavioral disorders in children. *Archives of Physical Medicine and Rehabilitation* 74:368–75.

Molnar, G.E., and J.C. Perrin. 1992. Head injury. In *Pediatric Rehabilitation* (2d ed.), edited by G. E. Molnar, 254–83. Baltimore: Williams & Wilkins.

Rivara, F. P., and B. A. Mueller. 1986. The epidemiology and prevention of pediatric head injury. *Journal of Head Trauma Rehabilitation* 1:7–15.

Teasdale, G., and B. Jennett. 1974. Assessment of coma and impaired consciousness: A practical scale. *Lancet* 2:81–84.

Thompson, R. S., F. P. Rivara, and D. C. Thompson. 1989. Case-control study of the effectiveness of bicycle safety helmets. *New England Journal of Medicine* 320:1361–67.

U.S. House of Representatives. 1990. *Individuals with Disabilities Education Act.* Public Law 101–476. Washington, D.C.

Gail

*Leadership and learning are
indispensable to each other.*

—J .F. Kennedy

Background

Gail had just returned from a continuing education seminar where the instructor discussed the theoretical rationale and demonstrated fabrication of popular orthotic designs for use with clients with central nervous system (CNS) dysfunction. Although therapists may provide orthotics for children with hypotonia or hypertonia, Gail was particularly interested in splinting two children with spasticity.

CNS dysfunction alters muscle tone that restricts movement, reduces coordination, and impacts on psychological health and functional performance. The problems caused by disturbed CNS motor control and sensation in children include (a) abnormal muscle tone, movement patterns, and limb position, (b) hand disregard, (c) excessive thumb flexion and adduction, and (d) muscular weakness, pain, and loss of range of motion due to structural changes of soft tissue or edema (Reid 1992). By reducing spasticity, orthotics prevent deterioration in joint and soft tissue integrity, facilitate more normal movement patterns, and promote functional independence. Therapists provide splints and orthotics to develop skill, restore function, maintain ability, and promote health (Canadian Association of Occupational Therapists 1987).

A number of neurological conditions produce spastic clinical pictures. Spasticity is a state of increased muscular tone and is characterized by hyperreflexia, hypertonia, and clonus (Chapman and Weisendanger 1982). Hyperreflexia is identified by an exaggerated phasic or tendon stretch reflex. Hypertonia describes increased resistance to passive movement (tonic stretch reflex). Rhythmically repeated muscle contractions, called *clonus,* can be elicited by quick and sustained muscle tension. Clonus is documented by its presence, duration, and the joint where it can be elicited. Clinically, it is often detected during quick, passive movement toward elbow extension, forearm supination, and foot dorsiflexion.

Although clinicians lack an objective evaluation tool for spasticity, some therapists classify spasticity into mild, moderate, and severe. Pederson (1969) defines *mild spasticity* as slight resistance to passive stretch at end ranges, *moderate spasticity* as early resistance to passive movement with sudden yielding, and *severe spasticity* as little or no movement. Pedretti and Zoltan (1990) define *mild, moderate, and severe spasticity* according to the level of reflex sensitivity, balance of tone, resistance to stretch, and functional movement. Carrasco (1989) defines *mild, moderate, and severe spasticity* in terms of quality and distribution of tone, range of motion (ROM), quality of movement, reflexes, and reactions. Bohannon and Smith (1986) proposed a *Modified Ashworth Scale* to document resistance to passive stretch that has shown to have good reliability. The *Movement Assessment of Infants* proposes a muscle tone evaluation scale to screen infants from birth to 12 months of age (Chandler et al. 1980).

Neurophysiological approaches to orthotic design incorporate the neuromuscular facilitation principles introduced by Margaret Rood (1956) and Berta and Karl Bobath (1978). Reflex inhibiting patterns, active and inactive fields, tactile stimulation of antagonists for reciprocal inhibition, neutral warmth, prolonged stretch, and pressure to specific areas of the tendon are common techniques. Orthotics that provide prolonged stretch are made to position joints at submaximal range (5–10 degrees less than available range) to avoid elicitation of the stretch reflex (Feldman 1990; Hill 1988).

The biomechanical rationale for orthotic design focuses on using a mechanical device to provide prolonged positioning to align joints and prevent deformity and pain (Langlois et al. 1989). Muscle fibre length, sarcomere length and number, and muscle spindle calibration can be "reset" by prolonged lengthening to increase the potential for extension (Tardieu et al. 1979). Prolonged stretch, as opposed to intermittent stretch, allows tissues to expand through cell division. Too great a mechanical force, too quickly, can cause tearing and scarring of tissue, resulting in further loss of elasticity. Functional positioning within orthotics prevents breakdown of skin, overstretch of antagonist muscle groups, contractures in muscle and other soft tissue, and loss of joint range and integrity.

Gail was fascinated with the results her colleagues had achieved using various splint designs. After discussing the treatment protocol used in these successful cases with the responsible therapists, Gail received a range of responses to her questions. She wondered which children benefit most from orthotics, which splint designs provided the best results, what type of wearing schedule was optimal, and what was the best way to measure outcomes. Gail had begun the clinical reasoning process that often leads to research questions. To gain more knowledge, Gail attended a seminar and conducted a literature search at the library.

One of Gail's colleagues suggested she read an article by Reid (1992), who surveyed 399 Canadian pediatric occupational therapists (60% response rate), and found that most pediatric therapists use the resting hand palmar splint (71%), followed by the thumb splint (65%), hard cone (50%), spasticity reduction splint (32%), and the inflatable splint (31%). (See Figures 5.22, 5.23, 5.24, 5.26, and 5.30.) When asked why they chose to use one of the three most popular designs, respondents indicated that "It works," and cited the ease of fabrication and increased client comfort. When asked why they didn't use certain designs, 30% of respondents indicated a lack of familiarity. Therapists who worked less than 5 years or received postgraduate training in splinting demonstrated the greatest tendency to splint, in comparison to those who had worked more than 5 years or had no special postgraduate training.

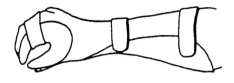

Figure 5.22 Resting Hand Palmar Splint

Figure 5.23 Thumb Splint (Short Opponens)

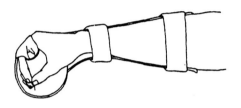

Figure 5.24 Hard Cone Splint
(Jamison and Dayhoff 1980; Rood 1956)

Figure 5.25 Spasticity Hand Splint
(Snook 1979)

Figure 5.26 Inflatable Splint
(Bloch and Evans 1977)

Most of the research on the effectiveness of orthotics as a treatment modality uses small sample descriptive studies with adults. The scarcity of research, methodological weaknesses of documented studies, and contradictory results add to the ongoing controversy regarding their effectiveness. Research design and methodology is difficult due to

- natural fluctuations with spasticity and its responsiveness to both emotional and systemic factors,
- the variance in symptomatology among clients with the same diagnosis,
- the lack of an objective tool to measure changes in spasticity,
- variable wearing compliance,
- the lack of comparison groups, and
- the diverse clinical nature of the people with CNS dysfunction

(Langlois et al. 1989).

146

After reviewing the journal literature from the library and the resource material available within the occupational therapy department, Gail completed her collection of anti-spasticity hand splint design illustrations. (See Figures 5.27–5.31.)

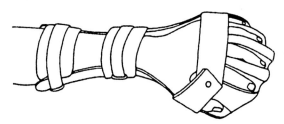

Figure 5.27 Anti-Spasticity Finger Spreader
(Adapted from Bobath 1981; Doubilet and Polkow 1977)

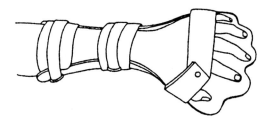

Figure 5.28 Anti-Spasticity Ball Splint

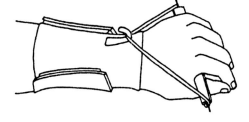

Figure 5.29 MacKinnon Splint

Adapted with permission of Canadian Association of Occupational Therapists (CAOT) Publications. MacKinnon, Sanderson, and Buchanan. 1975. *Canadian Journal of Occupational Therapy.* The MacKinnon Splint: A functional hand splint: 42:157-58.

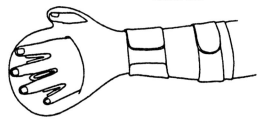

Figure 5.30 Spasticity Reduction Splint

Adapted with permission of The American Journal of Occupational Therapy. Spasticity reduction splint by J. H. Snook. Copyright by the American Occupational Therapy Association, Inc.

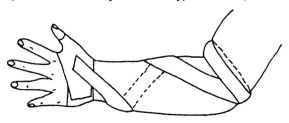

Figure 5.31 Thumb Abductor Supinator Splint

Reprinted with permission. Casey, C., and E. J. Kratz. 1988. Soft splinting with neoprene: The thumb abductor supinator splint. *The American Journal of Occupational Therapy* 42(6), Figure 2, p. 396.

Gail decided that it was time to make some clinical decisions. It seemed that some orthotics incorporated more aggressive techniques than others. Some orthotics could be used during functional activities, and others could not. Gail thought that it was appropriate to use different orthotics for different levels of severity of spasticity and for different purposes. She also could change the design as the child developed. Splinting and casting, like all other treatment modalities, would be tailor-designed to meet identified client needs. According to Feldman (1990), clinicians should be clear about the treatment goals of patients and should not automatically treat contractures or spasticity just because they are present.

Gail thought of two children on her caseload—Natalie and Ali.

Natalie

Natalie is almost 10 years old. She was diagnosed with mild right hemiplegic cerebral palsy (CP) at 1 year and had received therapy on and off throughout her life. As a recent graduate of the 4th grade, she has little difficulty at school. Her leisure interests include crafts, swimming, and dancing. Although self-help skills were difficult when she was younger, Natalie indicates that she no longer needs therapy in this area. Her mother, however, continues to manage Natalie's hair accessories, shoelaces, and earrings. Although Natalie has not been seen for therapy for the past 2 years, she requests that occupational therapy help her improve her swimming stroke to pass beginner lessons, learn to skip with a rope, and participate in difficult school art projects such as origami and string art. The mild spasticity in Natalie's right arm and hand make these activities very difficult.

Natalie is able to pick up a 1-inch button, a pencil, and an eraser from the tabletop with her right hand. She has extreme difficulty retrieving pennies and small beads from the table. When asked to grasp an object, Natalie reaches with slight wrist flexion and ulnar deviation, metacarpal phalangeal (MP) extension, slight interphalangeal (IP) flexion, and excessive thumb flexion and adduction. This adduction and loss of opposition interferes with functional two-point or three-point tip-and-pad pinch. Gail recalls reading that the thumb carpal metacarpal (CMC) joint, in children with web space contractures, must be controlled to prevent ulnar collateral ligament stretch or rupture (Phelps and Weeks 1976). She wonders about the condition of Natalie's CMC joint.

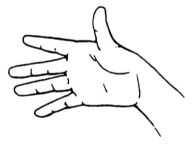

Figure 5.32 Natalie's Hand

148

When she is tired or involved in strenuous activities, Natalie holds her right thumb within her palm. Although her muscle tone is typically less during sleep, her thumb remains adducted. Natalie's upper extremity (U/E) active joint range of motion (ROM) measurements, while sitting in a chair, are delineated in Table 5.1.

Ali

Ali is a 6-year-old boy who was in a motor vehicle accident 2 years ago. His motor skills are influenced by a moderate-level spastic quadriplegia and some clonus. Due to frequent and excessive pelvic thrusting, Ali uses a special wheelchair seating system. Ali uses a single switch to play with his toys. He has a number of friends at school and within his community. He does not follow verbal instructions, and Gail doubts whether Ali could verbalize discomfort or pain. His father indicates that Ali communicates his wishes with smiles.

Ali holds his arms predominantly in a flexor synergy with elbow flexion, forearm pronation, wrist flexion and ulnar deviation, finger and thumb flexion/adduction. To activate his switch or reach out for his father, Ali uses an extensor U/E synergy pattern. Passive ROM was limited, as delineated in Table 5.1.

Table 5.1 Natalie and Ali's Upper Extremity Range of Motion Measurements

Natalie's Right U/E Active ROM	Joint Range of Motion			Ali's Passive ROM	
				Right	Left
110°	Shoulder	Flexion	0°–180°	120°	110°
80°		Abduction	0°–180°	100°	90°
10°–120°	Elbow	Extension-Flexion	0°–150°	20°–150°	0°–100°
20°		Supination	0°– 80°	20°	0°
full		Pronation	0°– 80°	full	full
full	Wrist	Flexion	0°– 80°	full	70°
10°		Extension	0°– 70°	30°	20°
30°		Ulnar Deviation	0°– 30°	30°	20°
0°		Radial Deviation	0°– 20°	0°	0°
~80°	Fingers	MP Ext-Flexion	0°– 90°	~20°–90°	~30°–70°
~30°–80°		Proximal IP Ext-Flexion	0°–100°	~30°–80°	~30°–80°
~20°–40°		Distal IP Ext-Flexion	0°– 90°	~30°–50°	~40°–50°
See Figure 5.32	Thumb	MP Ext-Flexion	0°– 50°	10°–50°	~20°–50°
		IP Ext-Flexion	+10– 80°	30°–80°	~30°–80°
		Abduction	0– 70°	30°	20°

~ denotes approximately

The Challenge

You are Gail. Natalie, her family, and Ali's parents have indicated that they would agree to using splints if the splints "help." Decide whether or not you will design an orthotic for each of these two children. If you do, which design is most appropriate? What wearing schedule and precautions will you provide these families? If you would like assistance with this challenge, use the questions and resources below to aid your analysis. Complete questions 3, 5–7, 9 and 11 at a minimum. See Selected Answers in Appendix E.

Questions to Aid Analysis

1. What is the neurological basis for spasticity? Describe flexor and extensor synergy patterns.

2. What is the Bobath reflex inhibiting pattern for the distal upper extremity? Which orthotics incorporate this strategy?

3. Describe the neurophysiological and biomechanical principles incorporated in each design. What do you think about the use of inhibitive casting?

	Neurophysiological Principles	Biomechanical Principles
Resting hand palmar		
Thumb splint		
Hard cone		
Spasticity reduction splint		
Inflatable splint		
Spasticity hand splint		
Anti-spasticity ball splint		
Dorsal wrist cock up		
Thumb abductor supinator		
Inhibitive casting		

4. At the neurological level, what is happening during prolonged stretch?

5. Answer the following questions for both Natalie and Ali. Use Coppard and Lohman (1996) for assistance.

   What is the goal(s) of treatment (develop skill, restore function, maintain ability, and promote health)?

   What joints would you want to include in your orthotic?

   What orthotic design(s) would help you meet these objectives?

   Would you make any special adaptations?

What thermoplastic properties will be important to fabricate this design (memory, drying time, rigidity, conformity, drape, elasticity)?

Which splinting material will you choose?

How will you measure change?

What wearing schedule would you recommend? Give consideration to research findings, tone quality and quantity, joint integrity, lifestyle, and potential compliance difficulties.

6. What information and precautions will need to be shared with the parents of these two children?

7. Do you need a medical referral for this treatment strategy? If so, be prepared to explain your rationale to the physician.

8. Assume that you have included Natalie's wrist within a thumb opponens splint, with forearm included to reduce her ulnar deviation, and her grasp pattern deteriorated? What are your options?

9. Hand orthoses facilitate and improve grasp or attempt to alter U/E muscle tone. What activities and treatment methods should Gail use to assist these children in improving their trunk, shoulder, and elbow function to enhance the quality and accuracy of reach and object placement?

10. What variables may influence the effectiveness of orthotics as a treatment modality? Do you have any research questions of your own? How would you design your research study?

11. What is your impression about the efficacy of orthotics as an adjunct to treatment in the neurologically impaired child?

New Terminology

AROM	hyperreflexia	ROM
clonus	hypertonia	spasticity
CNS	hypotonia	TBI
dorsal	phasic stretch reflex	tonic stretch reflex
electromyelogram	PROM	volar
goniometer	sarcomere	

Learning Resources

Coppard, B. M., and H. Lohman. 1996. *Introduction to splinting: A critical thinking and problem-solving approach.* St. Louis: C. V. Mosby.

Hill, S. G. 1988. Appendix A: Current trends in upper extremity splinting. In *Improving upper body control, Checklist for hand splints,* edited by R. Boehme, 139. Tucson, AZ: Therapy Skill Builders.

Langlois, S., J. R. MacKinnon, and L. Pederson. 1989. Hand splints and cerebral spasticity: A review of the literature. *Canadian Journal of Occupational Therapy* 56:113–19.

Neuhaus, B., E. Asher, B. Coullon, M. Donohue, A. Einbond, J. Glover, S. Goldberg, and V. Takai. 1981. A survey of rationales for and against hand splinting in hemiplegia. *American Journal of Occupational Therapy* 35:83–90.

Reid, D. T. 1992. A survey of Canadian occupational therapists' use of hand splints for children with neuromuscular dysfunction. *Canadian Journal of Occupational Therapy* 59:16–27.

Yasukawa, A. 1990. Upper extremity casting: Adjunct treatment for a child with cerebral palsy hemiplegia. *American Journal of Occupational Therapy* 44:840–46.

Many of the splints described in this case are available from the following providers:

North Coast Medical, Inc.
187 Stauffer Boulevard
San Jose, CA 95125-1042
1-800-821-9319

Smith & Nephew Rolyan, Inc.
One Quality Drive
P.O. Box 1005
Germantown, WI 53022
1-800-558-8633

Sammons
P.O. Box 386
Western Springs, IL 60558-0386
1-800-323-5547

Focus on Research

Table 5.2 Research on the Effectiveness of Splinting and Casting Spastic Upper Extremities (1960–1994)

Study	Subjects	Orthoses	Measuring Device	Results
Kaplan 1962	10 hemiplegic adults Age: 28–70	Dorsal splint; worn for an average of 8 hours/day for 20 weeks.	Goniometer Electromyelogram (EMG) Muscle strength Functional evaluation	Mean increase wrist range = 76° Minimal improvement strength
Zislis 1964	1 female	Dorsal and volar splints.	EMG	Less flexor EMG with volar than dorsal or no splint.
Charait 1968	20 post-CVA Age: 30–80	Dorsal and volar splints; worn for 2 months to 3 years for 2–23 hours per day.	Clinical observation	Dorsal more effective than volar.
Dayhoff 1975	3 post-CVA Age: 75–84	Cone splint; worn during the day.	Dynamometer Clinical observation	"Positive clinical effects" with maximum improvement by 6 weeks.

continued

Table 5.2 Research on the Effectiveness of Splinting and Casting Spastic Upper Extremities (1960–1994)
(continued)

Study	Subjects	Orthoses	Measuring Device	Results
MacKinnon et al. 1975	31 children	MacKinnon splint	Clinical observation of hand awareness, use, acceptance, and decreased spasticity.	"Excellent results."
Doubilet and Polkow 1977	15 post-CVA	Finger abduction splint; worn during the day.	Clinical observation	Moderate reduction in spasticity after 1 week.
Snook 1979	18 hemi- plegic or TBI	Snook spasticity reduction splint; inter- mittent wearing schedules.	Clinical observation	Immediate and marked reduction of tone in hand and entire upper extremity.
Jamison and Dayhoff 1980	11 post-CVA Age: 58–96	Cone splint for 24 hours/day for 28 days.	Goniometer Dynamometer Functional evaluation	Statistically signifi- cant reduction hypertonia. Most marked change after 1 week. Greatest decrease in younger versus older. Only slight changes in function.
McPherson 1981	5 severe and profoundly handicapped Age: 10–18	Snook spasticity reduction splint; worn for 5 weeks with progressive 15 min- ute increase/week.	Spring-weighted scale	Statistically signifi- cant reduction in hypertonus after 4 weeks. Decreased tone as wearing time increased. Effects not permanent.
McPherson et al. 1982	10 CVA, TBI, CP Age: 24–76	Dorsal and volar splint; worn for 12 hours/day for 5 weeks.	Spring-weighted scale	Splinting reduces hypertonicity. No statistically signifi- cant difference. Spasticity levels increase with age.

continued

153

Table 5.2 Research on the Effectiveness of Splinting and Casting Spastic Upper Extremities (1960–1994) (continued)

Study	Subjects	Orthoses	Measuring Device	Results
Exner and Bonder 1983	12 hemi-plegic CP Age: 3–16	Cross-over design with orthokinetic cuff, short opponens splint, and MacKinnon splint; worn for 8 hours daily for 6 weeks with 2 week intervals between splints.	Photography and formulated observational tests to measure bilateral hand use, grasp, and arm-hand posture.	No significant relationship between splint type and variables measured. MacKinnon splint most preferred by parents and clients, and more likely associated with improved bilateral hand use and grasp skill.
Mathiowetz et al. 1983	8 normal and 5 hemiplegic	Resting hand splint, hard cone, finger spreader, and no device.	EMG	No significant reduction in EMG with any device.
Mills 1984	18	Bivalve splint; worn for 2 hours.	EMG Goniometer	EMG increase in 7 limbs; increased in 3. No statistically significant increase in joint range.
McPherson et al. 1985	4 men and 4 women 1 year post-CVA. Age: 67–86	Dynamic dorsal splint; worn for 1 hour 3 days/week for 6 weeks.	Spring-weighted scale	Statistically significant reduction in hypertonus in splinted, but not in PROM control group.
Scherling et al. 1989	18 post-CVA	Dorsal dynamic wrist-hand orthosis; worn for 16 to 22 hours.	Clinical observations	Varying degrees of wrist and hand tone reduction. Minimum 4 hour/day wearing. Carry-over effect for $1/2$ to 3 hours after orthotic removal.

continued

154

Table 5.2 Research on the Effectiveness of Splinting and Casting Spastic Upper Extremities (1960–1994)
(continued)

Study	Subjects	Orthoses	Measuring Device	Results
Langlois et al. 1991	9 hemi-plegic post-CVA	Finger spreader splint and self ROM; splint worn for either 22, 12, or 6 hours/day for 4 weeks.	Torque motor system. Expectation and satisfaction questionnaires	Reduction in spasticity of all groups. No significant differences among wearing schedules. No significant differences between prescribed schedule and reported compliance. Significant correlation between outcome expectation and reported compliance.
Reid and Sochaniwskyj 1992	10 CP children Age: 5–12	Hand splint (similar to MacKinnon splint); worn for 1½ weeks.	EMG Motion analysis Visual motor tests	Majority of children demonstrated increased quality of movement.
Hill 1994	15 TBI Age: 9–48	Cross-over design with casts worn continuously versus traditional techniques and splinting.	Goniometer Range where stretch reflex is elicited. Functional tasks. Evaluated after both 1 and 2 months of treatment.	Casting was more effective in reversing contracture and clinical indications of spasticity, but no significant improvement in functional skills.

Adapted with permission from Tables 1–3. Langlois, S, J., R. MacKinnon, and L. Pederson. 1989. Hand splints and cerebral spasticity: A review of the literature. *Canadian Journal of Occupational Therapy* 56:115–117.

References

Bloch, R., and M. G. Evans. 1977. An inflatable splint for the spastic hand. *Archives of Physical Medicine and Rehabilitation* 58:179–80.

Bobath, B. 1978. *Adult hemiplegia: Evaluation and treatment.* London: William Heinemann Medical Books.

Bobath, B. 1981. *Adult hemiplegia: Evaluation and treatment.* 2d ed. London: William Heinemann Medical Books.

Bohannon, R. W., and M. B. Smith. 1986. Interrater reliability of a modified Ashworth Scale of muscle spasticity. *Physical Therapy* 67:206–7.

Canadian Association of Occupational Therapists. 1987. *Position paper on the use of orthoses in occupational therapy.* Toronto: Canadian Association of Occupational Therapists.

Carrasco, R. C. 1989. Children with cerebral palsy. In *Occupational therapy for children-2d ed.,* edited by P. N. Pratt and A. S. Allen, 396–421. St. Louis: C. V. Mosby.

Casey, C., and E. J. Kratz. 1988. Soft splinting with neoprene: The thumb abductor supinator splint. *American Journal of Occupational Therapy* 42:395–98.

Chandler, L. S., M. S. Andrews, and M. W. Swanson. 1980. *Movement assessment of infants: Manual.* Rolling Bay, WA: P.O. Box 4631.

Chapman, E., and M. Wiesendanger. 1982. The physiological and anatomical basis of spasticity: A review. *Physiotherapy Canada* 34:125–35.

Charait, S. 1968. A comparison of volar and dorsal splinting of the hemiplegic hand. *American Journal of Occupational Therapy* 22:319–21.

Citta-Pietrolungo, T. J., M. A. Alexander, and N. L. Steg. 1992. Early detection of heterotopic ossification in young patients with traumatic brain injury. *Archives of Physical Medicine and Rehabilitation* 73:258–62.

Dayhoff, N. 1975. Re-thinking stroke soft or hard devices to position hands. *American Journal of Occupational Therapy* 32:320–22.

Doubilet, L., and L. Polkow. 1977. Theory and design of a finger abduction splint for the spastic hand. *American Journal of Occupational Therapy* 31:320–22.

Exner, C., and B. Bonder. 1983. Comparative effects of three hand splints on bilateral hand use, grasp, and arm-hand posture in hemiplegic children: A pilot study. *Occupational Therapy Journal of Research* 3:75–92.

Feldman, P. A. 1990. Upper extremity casting and splinting. In *The practical management of spasticity in children and adults,* edited by M. B. Glenn, and J. Whyte, 149–66. Philadelphia: Leas & Febiger.

Hill, J. 1988. Appendix B: Casting to improve upper extremity function. In *Improving upper body control,* edited by R. Boehme. Tucson, AZ: Therapy Skill Builders.

Hill, J. 1994. The effects of casting on upper extremity motor disorders after brain injury. *American Journal of Occupational Therapy* 48:219–24.

Hurvitz, E. A., B. R. Mandac, G. Davidoff, J. H. Johnson, and V. S. Nelson. 1992. Risk factors for heterotopic ossification in children and adolescents with severe traumatic brain injury. *Archives of Physical Medicine and Rehabilitation* 73(May):459–62.

Jamison, S., and N. Dayhoff. 1980. A hard hand-positioning device to decrease wrist and finger hypertonicity: A sensorimotor approach for the patient with non-progressive brain damage, *Nursing Research* 29:285–89.

Kaplan, N. 1962. Effect of splinting of reflex inhibition and sensorimotor stimulation in the treatment of spasticity. *Archives of Physical Medicine and Rehabilitation* 43:565–69.

Langlois, S., J. R. MacKinnon, and L. Pederson. 1989. Hand splints and cerebral spasticity: A review of the literature. *Canadian Journal of Occupational Therapy* 56:113–19.

Langlois, S., L. Pederson, and J. R. MacKinnon. 1991. The effects of splinting on the spastic hemiplegic hand: Report of a feasibility study. *Canadian Journal of Occupational Therapy* 58:17–25.

MacKinnon, J., E. Sanderson, and J. Buchanan. 1975. The MacKinnon splint: A functional hand splint. *Canadian Journal of Occupational Therapy* 42:157–58.

Mathiowetz, V., D. Bolding, and C. Trombly. 1983. Immediate effects of positioning devices on the normal and spastic hand measured by electromyography. *American Journal of Occupational Therapy* 37:247–54.

McPherson, J. 1981. Objective evaluation of a splint designed to reduce hypertonicity. *American Journal of Occupational Therapy* 35:189–94.

McPherson, J., A. Becker, and N. Franszczak. 1985. Dynamic splint to reduce the passive component of hypertonicity. *Archives of Physical Medicine and Rehabilitation* 66:249–52.

McPherson, J., D. Kreimer, M. Aalderks, and T. Gallagher. 1982. A comparison of dorsal and volar resting hand splints in the reduction of hypertonus. *American Journal of Occupational Therapy* 36:664–70.

Mills, V. 1984. Electromyographic results of inhibitory splinting. *Physical Therapy* 64:190–93.

Pederson, E. 1969. Clinical aspects of spasticity. In *Spasticity: Mechanisms, measurement, and management.* Springfield, IL: Charles C. Thomas.

Pedretti, L., and B. Zoltan. 1990. *Occupational therapy: Practice skills for physical dysfunction 3d Ed.* St. Louis: C. V. Mosby.

Phelps, R. E., and P. M. Weeks. 1976. Management of thumb-index web space contracture. *American Journal of Occupational Therapy* 30:543–50.

Reid, D. T. 1992. A survey of Canadian occupational therapists' use of hand splints for children with neuromuscular dysfunction. *Canadian Journal of Occupational Therapy* 59:16–27.

Reid, D. T., and A. Sochaniwskyj. 1992. Influences of a hand positioning device on upper extremity control of children with cerebral palsy. *International Journal of Rehabilitation Research* 15:15–29.

Rood, M. S. 1956. Neurophysiological mechanisms utilized in the treatment of neuro-muscular dysfunction. *American Journal of Occupational Therapy* 4:220–25.

Scherling, E., and H. Johnson. 1989. A tone-reducing wrist-hand orthosis. *American Journal of Occupational Therapy* 43:609–11.

Snook, J. 1979. Spasticity reduction splint. *American Journal of Occupational Therapy* 33:648–51.

Tardieu, C., P. Tardieu, P. Colbeau-Justin, E. Huet de la Tour, and A. Lespargot. 1979. Trophic muscle regulation in children with congenital cerebral lesions. *Journal of Neurological Sciences* 42:357–64.

Zislis, J. 1964. Splinting of the hand in a spastic hemiplegic patient. *Archives of Physical Medicine and Rehabilitation* 45:41–43.

Appendix A

Assessments Used by Pediatric Occupational Therapists

Test	Use	Features
Alberta Infant Motor Scale (AIMS) Piper, M., and J. Darrah 1994.	0–18 months To screen and identify at-risk infants and evaluate over time	Normed sample of 2,000 in 1990–92 Test-observer reliability = 0.99 Test-retest reliability = 0.99 Concurrent validity = 0.98 Bayley Scales and 0.97 with PDMS Observational assessment Manual is a text entitled *Movement Assessment of the Developing Infant.*
Batelle Developmental Inventory (BDI) Newborg, J., J. R. Stock, L. Wnek, J. Guidubaldi, and J. Svinicki 1988.	Birth–8 years Assesses: Personal-social Adaptive Motor Communication Cognition	Stratified national sample of 800 Observation and interview Full assessment and screening editions Limited sensitivity for 0 to 3 age range
Bayley Scales of Infant Development II (Second Edition) (Bayley II) Bayley, N. 1993.	1–42 months Screens: Mental Psychomotor Behavior Rating	Normed sample of 1,700 across the U.S. using 1988 U.S. census data Interrater reliability > 0.89 Test-retest reliability > 0.75 Measures milestones, not quality of movement High correlation: *Stanford-Binet* Evaluator-elicited responses

Test	Use	Features
Bayley Infant Neuro-developmental Screener (BINS) Aylward, G. 1995.	3–24 months Screens: Auditory reception Visual reception Verbal expression Motor Cognitive	Normed sample of more than 900 clinical and non-clinical infants Interrater reliability = 0.70 to 0.96 Test-retest reliability = 0.71 to 0.84 Internal consistency = 0.73 to 0.85 Cut scores provided at monthly age intervals to determine low, moderate, and high-risk status Specificity = 2%–6%. Administration time 5–10 minutes
Bruinicks-Oseretsky Test of Motor Proficiency (BOTMP) Bruininks, R. 1978.	4.5–14.5 years Diagnostic assessment: Gross Motor Fine Motor	Normed sample of 765 (1970 U.S. Census) Interrater reliability (subtest 7) = 0.90 to 0.98 Test-retest reliability = 0.86 to 0.89 SEM = 4–5 standard score points Full assessment and screening editions
Clinical Observations of Motor and Postural Skills (COMPS) Wilson, B, N. Pollock, B. Kaplan, and M. Law 1994.	5–9 years Screens for subtle motor coordination problems	Research sample of 123, including 67 children with developmental coordination disorder and 56 with no known motor problems Interrater reliability 0.77 to 0.88 with therapists and 0.72 occupational therapy students Test-retest reliability exceeded 0.75 when administered within 2 weeks Sensitivity 82%–100%. Specificity 63%–90% Administration time 15–20 minutes
Canadian Occupational Performance Measure (COPM) Law, M., S. Baptiste, A. Carswell, M.A. McColl, H. Polatajko, and N. Pollock 1994.	All ages and diagnostic categories Identifies and evaluates client's self-perception of occupational perform-ance. Useful for outcome evaluation.	Development and testing sample of 268 individu-als in Canada, New Zealand, Greece, and Britain Test-retest reliability = 0.63 for performance and 0.84 for satisfaction Administration requires knowledge of the Model of Occupational Performance, as articulated in the Canadian *Guidelines for Client-Centred Practice*
The Carolina Curriculum Johnson-Martin, N., K. Jens, S. Attermeier, and B. Hecker 1991.	Birth–5 years Curriculum-based assessment: Cognition Communication Social Adaptation Fine and Gross Motor	Field-tested in 22 programs for 3 months Infant and toddler edition (0–24 months) Preschooler edition (2–5 years) Provides graphic system for data charting, and includes intervention strategies Specifies adaptations for children with disabilities
Denver II Frankenburn, W., and J. Dodds 1990.	1–72 months Screens: Personal-social Fine motor-adaptive Language Gross motor	Normed sample of 2,096 in Denver area using 1990 U.S. census data. Not random or stratified. Interrater reliability = 0.99 Test-retest reliability = 0.90

Test	Use	Features
Developmental Test of Visual Motor Integration (Third Edition) (VMI-R) Beery, K.E. 1989.	2.5 years–19 years Screens visual motor integration, using paper and pencil reproduction of geometric forms.	Normed sample of 5,824 children representative of 1980 US census data Interrater reliability = 0.93 Test-retest reliability = 0.81 Split-half = 0.85 Correlation with handwriting = 0.42; academic readiness = 0.50; chronological age = 0.89; and WISC-R = 0.49 Some predictive ability with young school-age children Standard score mean = 100, SD = 15 Fourth revision due in 1996
Early Learning Accomplishment Profile (E-LAP) Glover, M., J. Preminger, and A. Sanford 1978.	0–36 months Development scales: Gross motor Fine motor Cognition Language Self-help Social-emotional	Based on information from normative evaluation tests No reliability or validity tests
Erhardt Developmental Prehension Assessment (EDPA) (2nd Edition) Erhardt, R. 1994.	0–72 months	Criterion-referenced theory, assessment and treatment protocol available in *Developmental Hand Dysfunction* (2nd Edition) Available from Therapy Skill Builders, San Antonio, TX
FirstSTEP Screening Test for Evaluating Preschoolers Miller, L. J. 1993.	2 years 9 months– 6 years 2 months Preschool screening: Cognitive Language Motor Optional screening: Social-emotional Adaptive behaviors Parent/teacher scale	Nationwide normed sample of 1,433 which reflects the same proportion of ethnic minorities as found in the 1988 U.S. Census survey Addresses the five domains of the *Individuals with Disabilities Education Act* Interrater reliability (Composite) = 0.91 Test-retest reliability (Composite) = 0.93 Identifies at-risk children = 72%–85% Specificity = 76%–83% Composite score highly correlated with MAP total score (r = 0.71) Construct, content and discriminative validity Administration time 15 minutes
Gesell Developmental Schedules (GDS) Knobloch, Stevens, and Malone 1980.	2–36 months Screens: Adaptive Gross and fine motor Language Personal-social-behavioral	Latest restandardization in 1980 Predictive validity with *Stanford-Binet* IQ at 3 years of age is high (r = 0.87)

Test	Use	Features
Hawaii Early Learning Profile-Revised (HELP-R) Furuno, S., K. A. O'Reilly, C. M. Hosaka, T. T. Inatsuka, B. Zeisloft, and T. Allman 1988.	0–36 months Development checklist: Cognition Language Gross motor Fine motor Social-emotional Self-help	Criterion-referenced, curriculum-based assessment designed to facilitate infant screening, and monitoring through multidisciplinary evaluation, and program planning Provides 650 age-referenced developmental milestones ages 0–3 Provides 625 age-referenced developmental milestones for ages 3–6 Revised checklist for 0–3 years in 1994 New checklist for 3–6 year olds
Milani-Comparetti Motor Development Screening Test (Third Edition) (MCMDS) Stubery, S., P. Dehne, J. Miedaner, and P. Romero 1992.	0–2 years Screens: Postural control Active movement Primitive reflexes Automatic reactions	Criterion referenced Test-retest and interrater reliability are moderate to high (Paban and Piper 1987; Stuber et al. 1989) Evaluator elicited responses Ten-minute administration time Administration results at 3 months of age is not predictive of developmental outcome at 1, 2, or 3 years (VanderLinden 1985)
Miller Assessment of Preschoolers (MAP) Miller, L. 1982.	2 years 9 months–5 years 8 months Assessment: Foundations Coordination Verbal Nonverbal Complex tasks	Normative sample = 1,200 Test-retest reliability = 0.81 Reliability = 0.98 Identified at-risk children = 80% Internal consistency = 0.79 Several validity studies are cited in this manual Optional supplemental observations
Motor-Free Visual Perceptual Test-Revised (MVPT-R) Colarusso, R., and D. Hammill 1996.	4–11 years Screens motor-free visual perception.	Standardized on 961 children in Georgia and North Carolina Test-retest reliability = 0.77 to 0.83 Correlations with measures of visual perception (median $r = 0.49$); intelligence (median $r = 0.31$); and school performance (median $r = 0.38$) Perceptual quotients (PQ) mean = 100, and $SD = 15$

Test	Use	Features
Movement Assessment of Infants (MAI) Chandler, L., M. Andrews, and M. Swanson 1980.	0–12 months Screens quality of movement: Muscle tone Primitive reflexes Automatic reactions Volitional movement	Criterion referenced Small sample normative data used to create 4- and 8-month-old profiles Interrater reliability (4-month scale) = 0.72 Test-retest (4 months scale) = 0.76 High false-positive rate = 65% if use cut-off risk score of 8 (Paban and Piper 1987) Identifies delays with 67%–96% accuracy; and identifies normal infants with 62%–78% accuracy (Harris 1987) Twice as sensitive as the *Bayley Motor Scale* in detecting early signs of cerebral palsy (Harris 1987) Volitional movement score (4-month profile) is best predictor of overall developmental outcome (Harris et al. 1984)
Peabody Developmental Motor Scales (PDMS) Folio, M. R., and R. R. Fewell 1983.	Birth–83 months Comprehensive assessment: Fine motor scale (FMS) Gross motor scale (GMS)	Nonrandom sample of 617 in 1981–82 Interrater = 0.97 GMS; 0.94 FMS Test-retest reliability = 0.95 GMS; 0.80 FMS Reliable only when performed on children without disabilities (DeGangi 1987) Norm and criterion referenced Moderate to high concurrent validity with *Bayley Motor Scale;* weak to moderate correlations with the *Miller Assessment of Preschoolers* No predictive validity (Hinderer et al. 1989; Palisano 1986; Palisano and Lydic 1984)
Pediatric Evaluation of Disability Inventory (PEDI) Haley, S., W. Coster, L. Ludlow, J. Haltwanger, and P. Andrellos 1989.	6–90 months Comprehensive assessment of capacity and performance: Self-care Mobility Social function	Normed sample of 412 children in the northeastern United States in 1990–1991, using 1980 U.S. census data Interrater reliability = 0.92 to 0.99 Validation sample of 102 children with disabilities Concurrent validity with *Batelle* and *Functional Independence Measure for Children* = 0.70 to 0.97 Norm and criterion referenced Three scales: functional skills, caregiver assistance, and modifications
Piers-Harris Children's Self-Concept Scale (PHCSCS) Piers, E. V., and D. B. Harris 1993.	8–18 years Assesses self-concept	Self perception of physical appearance and attributes, intellectual and scholastic status, happiness and satisfaction, anxiety, behavior and popularity Individual and group administration

Test	Use	Features
Quick Neurological Screening Test (QNST) Mutti, M., H. Sterling, and N. Spalding 1978.	5–17 years Screens learning disabilities	Normed sample of 2,239, including 1,008 learning disabled (LD) subjects Test-retest reliability = 0.81 Interrater reliability = 0.71 Identifies normal with 93% accuracy Identifies LD with 70% accuracy Moderate correlation with *Bender-Gestalt,* and *Wide Range Achievement Tests* Not predictive
Sensory Integration and Praxis Tests (SIPT) Ayres, A. J. 1989.	4 years–8 years 11 months Assesses visual, tactile, and kinesthetic perception, as well as motor performance	National sample of 2,000 Computerized scoring Requires training in administration and interpretation Strong predictive validity for academic achievement (Parham 1989)
Test of Gross Motor Development (TGMD) Ulrich, D.A. 1985.	3–10 years Assesses motor skills: Locomotor skills Object control skills	Normed sample of 909 children from eight states, using 1980 U.S. census Norm and criterion referenced Test-retest reliability = 0.96 to 0.97 Interrater reliability = 0.94 to 0.97
Toddler and Infant Motor Evaluation (T.I.M.E.) Miller, L., and G. Roid 1994.	4–42 months Diagnostic assessment: Mobility Stability Motor organization Social/emotional Functional performance	National sample of 730 children from 1992 to 1993. Interrater reliability 0.90 to 0.99 Test-retest reliability 0.96 to 0.99 Decision consistency subtest ranges from 85%–100% Parent interview, elicited play, and natural observation
DeGangi-Berk Test of Sensory Integration (TSI) Berk, R., and G. DeGangi 1994.	3–5 years Screens: Postural control Bilateral integration Reflex integration	Criterion referenced Interrater reliability = 0.77 to 0.79 Test-retest reliability = 0.95 Total scores = 81% accuracy rate False normal error of only 9%

Test	Use	Features
Test of Visual Motor Skills (TVMS-R) Gardner, M. F. 1995.	3 years–13 years 11 months Assesses the ability to reproduce motorically what the subject visually perceives (visual motor). TVMS-R categorizes errors into 8 domains: closure; angles; inter-secting, and/or overlapping lines; size or port of form; rotation or reversal; line length; overpenetration or underpenetration; and modification of form.	Standardized sample of 1,334 subjects in the San Francisco Bay area. Split-half reliability = 0.92 Split-half reliability = 0.92 SEM for scaled scores = 0.85 SEM for standard scores = 4.24 Total score correlation with VMI-0.51; *Bender Gestalt Test* = 0.50 TVMS = 2–13 years TVMS-upper level (UL) = 12–40 years Can be administered in groups
Test of Visual Perceptual Skills (Non-Motor) (TVPS) Gardner, M. F. 1988.	4–19 years Diagnostic assessment of visual: Discrimination Memory Spatial relations Form constancy Sequencing memory Figure ground Closure	Standardized sample of 1,200 in the San Francisco Bay area TVPS edition = 4–13 years TVPS-upper level (UL) = 12–19 years Low internal reliability with good total test reliability (0.83 to 0.92) Moderate correlation with *Bender Visual Motor Gestalt* and VMI tests Low correlation with reading and spelling on *Wide Range Achievement Tests*
Vineland Adaptive Behavior Scale (VABS) Sparrow, S., D. Balla, and D. Cicchetti 1984.	Birth to adulthood Comprehensive assessment: Communication Daily living skills Socialization Motor skills	National sample of 3,000 from birth to 18 years 11 months to represent 1980 U.S. census information. Supplemental norms for people with disabilities Test-retest reliability = 0.81 to 0.86 Interrater reliability = 0.62 to 0.78 Three editions: Interview and survey Expanded interview Classroom
Functional Independence Measure for Children (WeeFim) Granger, C. V., and B.B. Hamilton 1992.	Thirteen motoric-based activities of daily-living skills and five cognitive items.	The FIM is used to determine the degree of disability that patients experience and the progress they make through programs in rehabilitation, by providing assessment and discharge measures of independence. FIM scores range from 0 = total assistance to 7 = complete independence. The WeeFIM is the pediatric version.

Assessment Supplier Information

American Guidance Service (AGS)
4201 Woodland Road
P.O. Box 99 (orders)
Circle Pines, MN 55014-1796
1-800-328-2560   (BOTMP) (VABS)

Academic Therapy Publications
20 Commercial Boulevard
Novato, CA 94949-6191
1-800-422-7249   (MVPT-R) (VMI)
                            (QNST) (TVPS)

Canadian Association of Occupational Therapists
Technology and Training Centre
Carlton University Campus
1125 Colonel By Drive, Ste. 3400
Ottawa, ON K1S 5R1
1-613-523-2268   (COPM)

DDM, Inc.
P.O. Box 6919
Denver, CO 80206-0919
1-303-355-4729   (*Denver II*)

Foundation for Knowledge in Development
1901 W. Littleton Blvd.
Littleton, CO 80120-2058
1-303-794-1182   (MAP)

Infant Movement Research
Box 4631
Rolling Bay, WA 98061   (MAI)

Modern Curriculum Press
4350 Equity Dr.
P. O. Box 2649
Columbus, OH 43216
1-800-321-3106   (VMI)

Modern Learning Press
P.O. Box 167
Rosemont, NJ 08556
1-800-627-5867   (GDS)

PEDI Research Group
Department of Rehabilitation Medicine
New England Medical Center Hospital
750 Washington Street 75K-R
Boston, MA 02111-1901
1-617- 636-5031   (PEDI)

PRO-ED
8700 Shoal Creek Boulevard
Austin, TX 78757-6897
1-512-451-3246
1-800-897-3202
1-800-397-7633 (FAX)   (TGMD) (VMI)

The Psychological Corporation
555 Academic Court
San Antonio, TX 78204-2498
1-800-228-0752   (*Bayley II*) (MAP)
                            (FirstSTEP)

Psychological and Educational Publications, Inc.
1477 Rollins Road
Burlingame, CA 94010-2316
1-800-523-5775   (QNST) (TVMS-R)
                            (TVPS)

Riverside Publishing Company
Houghton Mifflin Co.
8420 Bryn Mawr Avenue
Chicago, IL 60631
1-800-656-8420   (BDI)
                            (*The Carolina Curriculum*)
                            (PDMS)

Sammons, Inc.
P.O. Box 471
Bolingbrook, IL 60440-5071
1-800-323-5547   (BOTMP) (TVMS)
                            (TVPS)

Slosson Educational Publications, Inc.
P.O. Box 280
East Aurora, NY 14050-0280
1-800-828-4800   (MVPT) (TVMS)
                                  (TVPS) (VMI)

Therapro
225 Arlington Street
Framingham, MA 01702-8723
1-800-257-5376   (HELP) (MVPT)
                                  (QNST) (TVMS)
                                  (TVPS)

Therapy Skill Builders,
a division of The Psychological Corporation
555 Academic Court
San Antonio, TX 78204-2498
1-800-228-0752   (COMPS) (EDPA)
                                  (*FirstSTEP*) (MAP)
                                  (T.I.M.E.) (HELP)

UDS Data Management Service
Center for Functional Assessment Research
SUNY South Campus
232 Parker Hall
Buffalo, NY 14214
1-716-829-2076   (WeeFim)

W. B. Saunders
101 E. Oak Street
Oakland, NJ 07436
1-201-337-4694   (AIMS)

Western Psychological Services
12031 Wilshire Boulevard
Los Angeles, CA 90025-1251
1-800-648-8857   (PHCSCS) (SIPT)
                                  (TSI) (TVMS)
                                  (MVPT) (VMI)
                                  (TVPS) (QNST)

References

DeGangi, G. A. 1987. Test reviews: Sensorimotor tests. In *A therapist's guide to pediatric assessment,* edited by L. King-Thomas, and B. J. Hacker, 143–226. Boston, MA: Little, Brown and Company.

Erhardt, R. P. 1994. *Developmental hand dysfunction: theory, assessment, and treatment.* 2d ed. Tucson, AZ: Therapy Skill Builders.

Harris, S. R., M. W. Swanson, M. S. Andrews, C. J. Sells, N. M. Robinson, and F. C. Bennett. 1984. Predictive validity of the Movement Assessment of Infants. *Developmental and Behavioral Pediatrics* 5:336–42.

Harris, S. R. 1987. Early detection of cerebral palsy: sensitivity and specificity of two motor assessment tools. *Journal of Perinatology* 7:11–15.

Hinderer, K. A., P. K. Richardson, and S. W. Atwater. 1989. Clinical implications of the *Peabody Developmental Motor Scales:* A constructive review. *Physical and Occupational Therapy in Pediatrics* 9:81–106.

Paban, M., and M. Piper. 1987. Early predictors on one year neurodevelopmental outcome for at-risk infants. *Physical and Occupational Therapy in Pediatrics* 7:17–34.

Palisano, R. J. 1986. Concurrent and predictive validities of the *Bayley Motor Scale* and the *Peabody Developmental Motor Scales*. *Physical Therapy* 66:1714–19.

Palisano, R. J., and J. S. Lydic. 1984. *The Peabody Developmental Motor Scales:* An analysis. *Physical and Occupational Therapy in Pediatrics* 4:69–75.

Parham, L. D. 1989. In American Occupational Therapy Association. 1991. Statement: Occupational therapy provision for children with learning disabilities and/or mild to moderate perceptual and motor deficits. *American Journal of Occupational Therapy* 45:1069–73.

Stuberg, W. A., P. J. White, J. A. Miedaner, and P. R. Dehn. 1989. Item reliability of the *Milani-Comparetti Motor Developmental Screening Test*. *Physical Therapy* 69:328–35.

VanderLinden, D. 1985. Ability of the Milani-Comparetti developmental examination to predict motor outcome. *Physical and Occupational Therapy in Pediatrics* 5:27–38.

Appendix B

Federal Legislation That Affects Pediatric Occupational Therapists in the United States

Date Enacted	Public Law	Accompanying Documents	
		House Report	Senate Report
November 1975	Education for All Handicapped Children P.L. 94–142	94–332	94–168
October 1986	Education of the Handicapped Amendments P.L. 99–457	99–860	99–315
October 1986	Rehabilitation Act Amendments P.L. 99–506	99–571	99–388
July 1990	Americans with Disabilities Act P.L. 101–336	101–485	101–116
October 1990	Education of the Handicapped Amendments Individuals with Disabilities Education Act (IDEA)* P.L 101–476	101–544	101–204

*IDEA reauthorization of discretionary programs pending (Parts C through G).

Order a free copy by calling or writing the following address:

Document Room
United States House of Representatives
Washington, DC 20515
1-202-225-3121

Appendix C

Interacting Elements in the Model of Occupational Performance*

A. Areas Of Occupational Performance

Self-Care

grooming	dressing	community living
hygiene	mobility	shopping
toileting	bathing	banking
feeding	driving	transportation

Productivity

play (children)
school work
paid work
volunteer work
homemaking

Leisure

hobbies	entertainment and social involvement
use of free time	creative activities
use of community resources	collecting activities
pets	nature interests
cultural interests	games
recreation and sport involvement	volunteering
clubs and groups	

---

*From *Guidelines for the Client-Centred Practice of Occupational Therapy*, Health Canada, 1983. Reproduced with permission of the Ministry of Supply and Services Canada, 1995.

B. Performance Components

Mental

- cognition (memory, orientation, concentration, intellect, insight, judgment, general knowledge)
- mood and affect (appropriateness)
- behavior (appropriateness, control)
- perception (awareness of reality, visual perception)
- thought content (clarity, appropriateness, organization, compulsiveness)
- emotional defenses (e.g., denial, projection)
- reaction/adaptation to dysfunction
- body image
- volition in thought and behavior

Physical

- range of motion
- strength and muscle tone of individual muscles or muscle groups, particularly as they apply to functional tasks such as reaching and climbing
- coordination, balance, presence of involuntary movements (e.g., tremor, spasticity, etc.)
- endurance
- sensation (testing of functional limitations due to sensory disturbances in touch, pain, pressure, vision, hearing, taste, vibration, proprioception, kinesthesis and stereognosis)
- appearance (deformity, oedema, markings—particularly in terms of the functions they affect)
- pain (quality of pain, phantom pain, referred pain)
- visual perception

Sociocultural

- involvement in community
- family relationships
- friendships
- effect of client problems on relationships with family and others

Spiritual

- sense of purpose in life
- source of inner motivation
- presence of a set of beliefs and a value system

C. Physical, Social, and Cultural Environment

In examining the person's environment, the therapist should consider a number of factors; some examples follow.

Physical Environment

- wheelchair accessibility indoors/outdoors
- location of bedroom, bathroom, kitchen, living area (distance, stairs, width of door frames)
- type and condition of flooring for mobility, space, shape and distance for reaching clothing, kitchen goods, etc. (e.g., energy conservation features)

Social Environment

- relative or significant others at home
- availability of assistance during day and/or night
- companionship available
- friends or other support persons
- transportation available

Cultural Environment

(system of beliefs, ideals, customs and values)

- interests of others in the household or friendship group
- expectations regarding work, leadership in family, role, behavior
- activities requiring participation for acceptance
- attitudes to sickness/disability
- remedies and approaches for sickness/disability (e.g., local medicine)

Appendix D

Standardized Test Results

Johan

Johan's Performance on the *Alberta Infant Motor Scale*

	Previous Items	**Credited**	**Subscale Score**
Prone	5	5	10
Supine	3	5	8
Sit	1	4	5
Stand	1	1	2

Total Score = 25   Percentile = 50

Approximate *Peabody Developmental Motor Scale* Results. Age Norm for Gross Motor (Score = 77) and Fine Motor (Score = 52) Total Raw Scores = 5 months AE. (Folio and Fewell 1983 Table N-6, N-7). AE = Age Equivalency.

	Raw Score	**Percentile 6 Months AE**	**Percentile 5 Months AE**
Reflexes	22	33	93
Balance	7	15	67
Nonlocomotor	11	20	6
Receipt and Propulsion	4	30	-
Gross Motor Total	-	-	-
Score	77	19	87
Grasping	24	4	63
Hand Use	11	7	48
Eye-Hand Coordination	17	26	99
Manual Dexterity	-	-	-
Fine Motor Total Score	52	6	65

Simon

Simon's Performance on the *FirstSTEP*

Domain	Domain Score	Number of SDs from the Mean	Percentile Rank Equivalent
Cognitive	8	- 0.67	25
Language	5	- 1.67	5
Motor	9	- 0.33	37
Social-Emotional	9	- 0.33	37
Adaptive Behavior	8	- 0.67	25
Parent/Teacher	3	- 2.33	1
Sum of Domain	22	N/A	N/A
Composite	42	- 0.5 to - 1.0	16 to 31

Domain score: mean = 10, SD = 3. Composite score: mean = 50, SD = 10 (Miller 1993).

Heidi

Heidi's Performance on the *Test of Visual-Perception Skills (Non-Motor)*

Subtest	Raw Score	Scaled Score	Perceptual Age	Percentile Rank
Visual Discrimination	7	9	5–10	37
Visual Memory	3	7	5–1	16
Visual Spatial Relations	2	4	4–1	2
Visual Form Constancy	5	9	5–11	37
Visual Sequential Memory	1	4	4–1	2
Visual Figure Ground	2	5	4–5	5
Visual Closure	4	9	5–7	37

Sum of Scaled Scores: 47
Perceptual Quotient: 76
Percentile Rank: 5
Median Perceptual Age: 5–1

Heidi's Performance on the *Test of Visual Motor Skills-Revised*

Test Results: Accurate (One) Characteristics
Total Accurate Raw Score: 71 Motor Age: 5–0
Standard Score: 55 Scales Score: 1 Percentile Score: 1 Stanine: 1

Error (Zero) Characteristics

Classifications	Total Error Raw Scores	Standard Scores	Scaled Scores	Percentile Ranks	Stanines
(1)	6	92	8	29	4
(2)	25	69	4	2	1
(3)	11	55	1	1	1
(4)	5	67	3	1	1
(5)	7	55	1	1	1
(6)	7	64	3	1	1
(7)	6	59	2	1	1
(8)	9	71	4	3	1

Classifications

Design	1	2	3	4	5	6	7	8	One Scores	Design
1	1	—	—	1	—	—	—	1	3	1
2	1	1/1	—	—	1	1	—	—	5	2
3	1	—	—	—	1	—	—	1/1	4	3
4	—	1	1/1	—	1	—	—	1	5	4
5	—	0	0/1	—	1	1/0	—	—	3	5
6	1/0	0/1	—	—	0	0	—	—	2	6

Tim

Tim's Performance on the *Clinical Observations of Motor and Postural Skills* (COMPS)

Subtest	Raw Score	Weighted Score
Slow Motion	6	1.32
Rapid Forearm Rotation	11	5.06
Finger-Nose Touching	5	0.15
Prone Extension	2	- 0.08
ATNR	7	- 0.49
Supine Flexion	4	1.16
	Total	7.12
	Minus Adjustment	8.54
	Weighted Total Score	-1.42

Robert

Robert's Performance on the *Motor-Free Visual Perceptual Test-Revised*

Chronological Age	8 years 1 month
Perceptual Age	(6–4) 6–8 (7–0)
Perceptual Quotient	84
Raw Score	27

Robert's Performance on the *Developmental Test of Visual Motor Integration*

Raw Score = 12
Age Equivalent = 6 years 3 months
Standard Score = 84
Percentile = 14

176

Appendix E

Selected Answers

Johan

2. Johan would be considered at biological risk secondary to prematurity, and environmental risk secondary to family stressors, adolescent parenting, and low socioeconomic status. Apgar is not an accurate predictor of the 1-year developmental outcome, and weight at 3 months is a better predictor of 12-month neurological status (Paban and Piper 1987).

4. Well Baby Centers often offer health promotion, preventive care, and medical supervision for children. Medical personnel could provide physical examinations, diagnostic tests, and immunizations. Counseling and developmental assessments may be provided by counselors, social workers, nurses, physical, and occupational therapists.

6. Johan's corrected age is 5 months 23 days. His scores on the AIMS (Piper and Darrah 1994) and PDMS (Folio and Fewell 1983) are included in Appendix D.

8. Four components: assimilation, accommodation, association, and differentiation. Assimilation refers to sensory reception, whereas accommodation is the motor response. Association requires integration of assimilation and accommodation and the process of relating present and past experiences. Differentiation is the process of determining pertinent behaviors (Gilfoyle et al. 1990).

   Johan has learned from experience that pulling a string that is attached to a toy will cause the toy to move. To reach for the string, he assimilates and discriminates visual information, accommodates through reach, associates visual information (string size and distance) and upper limb proprioception with motoric reaching response to develop efficient reach. This information will be used again to differentiate movement patterns for more efficient future reach and grasp.

10. Maria and Barbara's assessment includes the subsystems of reflex integration, sensorimotor development, and spontaneous movement competencies. Evaluations that occur in familiar settings with favorite toys and the use of Mother to position and play with this child are congruent with contemporary views that meaningful context elicits more purposeful activity.

12. There is little evidence in this case indicating a need for intervention by an occupational therapist.

14. Johan continues to be at environmental risk. Environmental risk management and monitoring can likely occur through the team at the Well Baby Clinic. Review literature findings located in the *Focus on Research* section.

Kari

2. Performance context includes physical, social, and cultural context. Children affect and are affected by their environment in complex ways. Physical variables to consider during evaluation and intervention include the materials and objects available. Social variables include socioeconomic status, family structure, and relationships. Cultural context will be determined by family values, beliefs, and customs. See Richardson et al. (1993) for discussion on social environment.

4. Review Puttkammer's (1994) chapter.

6. Multidisciplinary teams benefit from professional specialization but lack interprofessional integration. Interdisciplinary teams collaborate for program planning and seek consensus on goals. Transdisciplinary teams collaborate on assessment and treatment, but only one individual implements the plan. These three approaches vary in their levels of role integration, service continuity, and complexity.

8. *Alberta Infant Motor Scale* (Piper and Darrah 1994)
   Battelle Developmental Inventory (Newborg et al. 1988)
   Bayley Infant Neurodevelopmental Screener (Aylward 1995)
   Denver II (Frankenburn and Dodds 1990)

10. Symptoms of NAS occur within the first few days and weeks of life and include neurologic, autonomic, gastrointestinal and respiratory signs. Irritability and restlessness, as well as disorganized suck, swallow, and poor feeding, are reasons for occupational therapy referral.

Antonio

2. Use HELP-R (Furuno et al. 1988) and *The Carolina Curriculum* (Johnson-Martin et al. 1991) to determine these competencies.

4. Some causes of cerebral palsy include (a) prenatal intracranial hemorrhage, brain anomalies, toxicosis and infections; (b) perinatal asphyxia and trauma; (c) and postnatal trauma, infections, hypoxia, metabolic disorders. Antonio has spastic hemiplegic cerebral palsy and would be considered as an established risk.

6. This chart has been started for you.

8. Antonio and his family would benefit from direct OT service. A biomechanical frame of reference is appropriate for seating, positioning, and bathtub equipment, while a motor control and/or neurodevelopmental frame of reference is appropriate for motor development. The *Toddler and Infant Motor Evaluation* (Miller and Roid 1994) would be appropriate for more advanced assessment.

10. The primary interventionist should serve as the case manager and coordinate the IFSP.

12. Provide your own suggestions.

14. Reauthorization still pending (1996).

Rozmin

2. Review these developmental theorists. Erikson's stage of Trust vs Mistrust and Piaget's sensorimotor cognitive stage (Coordination of Secondary Schema) must be considered during assessment and intervention planning. This cognitive level will influence the splint strap design and compliance.

4. Hypertrophic scar tissue has increased contractile properties, reduced tensile strength, and is hyperemic. Increased contractile properties require intervention to produce a flat and pliable scar and to prevent skin contracture and maintain joint integrity. Reduced tensile strength results in less tissue tolerance for shearing forces. Wound maturation will take from one to two years. Involvement of subcutaneous glands will necessitate the need for external lubricants. Refer to Jordan and Allely, 1996, p. 616.

6. Rozmin will require intervention in the joints that have lost range (right hip, knee, ankle, elbow, wrist, hand; left hip, ankle, wrist, and 5th digit). Prophylactic monitoring will be required at the joints that are at risk for contractures but have not yet lost range. Joints that should be positioned in anti-deformity positions are defined by Jordan and Allely, 1996, p. 620.

   Range of movement must be gained or maintained through active or passive movement and positioning. Active movement can be facilitated through purposeful, therapeutic activities. Splints provide positioning and must be worn as much as tolerated. Splint use decreases as active movement increases and may be worn just at nighttime before being discontinued. Caregivers must monitor skin for signs of irritation. Splints and garments must be cleaned at least twice daily during acute phases and daily in the rehabilitation phase. Splints will be terminated once full range of motion is attained and maintained or when the scar tissue has matured.

8. The skin under pressure garments and positioning modalities must be monitored for irritation. Improperly applied or cleaned garments and splints can cause skin irritation. Lubrication creams can cause allergic reactions. Children must not scratch new scar tissue.

10. All treatment activities must be goal-directed, meaningful, and appropriate for age and culture (AOTA 1993a). For example, elbow and wrist active extension can occur during an activity that requires crawling.

12. Pediatric rehabilitation requires that clinicians be sensitive to the resources, needs, and values of the family. The core values of equality, freedom of choice and self direction, dignity for the inherent worth and uniqueness of all individuals, and

prudence through judiciousness and discretion will be required with Rozmin's mother as with any other client family. Parents may need to learn how to interact with their child because they are afraid of the medical aspects of burn care (e.g., feeding tubes, dressings, etc.). Finally, health professionals may need to advocate for the burned child.

14. Outpatient and home health therapists will be responsible to manage Rozmin and her family's care through the rehabilitation phase of recovery. Attention to skin care, ensuring the proper use and application of garments and promoting independence and psychosocial recovery, will be required.

Simon (Part 1)

2. The *FirstSTEP* (Miller 1993) includes an optional Parent/Teacher Scale. The COPM (Wilson et al. 1994) is also an appropriate tool to establish and prioritize parent goals and objectives before or after you have been able to share specific assessment findings. Sonya and Simon's day-care workers have already established a relationship with this family and may also have insight into their concerns. You could use this information to start or continue conversations with these parents. The extended family members also may play an important role in the establishment of goals and objectives.

4. Motor (-0.33 standard deviations (SD) from the mean) and social-emotional (-0.33 SD) domain scores are within acceptable limits. Cognitive (-0.67 SD) and adaptive behavior (-0.67 SD) scores are below acceptable limits but not so poor as to warrant definite referral. The language (-1.67 SD) domain and responses on the Parent/Teacher Scales (-2.23 SD) indicate performance that is at the 5th and 1st percentile rank, respectively. The composite score of 42 is close to one standard deviation below the mean (mean = 50, SD = 10). Refer to Miller (1993, pp. 106–110) to interpret results and understand the color-code system.

Simon (Part 2)

2. Simon's foundations Index and Non-Verbal Index on the MAP (Miller 1988) are average or above average. Performance on Complex Tasks and Coordination Indices are 31 and 14 percent respectively, while the Verbal Index score is 3 percent. These percentile ranks indicate the percentage of children in the normative age group sample who obtained a score at or below Simon's score.

4. Recommendations, intervention, or consultation programs must follow family identified priorities. Completion of the *FirstSTEP* (Miller 1993) and MAP (Miller 1988) will assist you in guiding your discussion with this family in the type of service occupational therapy can provide to improve Simon's performance in adaptive behaviors and in addressing the concerns identified in the Parent/Teacher Scale. You may need to advocate for a speech therapy referral. As an occupa-

tional therapist, you also will be able to use these test results to determine the performance component areas that require attention (e.g., coordination and complex tasks) should occupational therapy intervention be requested by this family.)

6. Use Sonya and the day-care workers to assist you in this process. Review Case-Smith (1993, pp. 5–24) and Meadows (1991).

8. Review Lynch and Hanson (1992, pp. 80–111).

Pierre

2. Performance is compared to the norm for evaluation purposes and to determine program and service eligibility.

4. Down's syndrome is caused by an additional chromosome 21, also called trisomy 21. The physical characteristics include short stature, small flattened head, upward slanting eyes and an enlarged tongue. Other features and related health problems include mental retardation, low body tone, hypermobile joints, cardiovascular anomalies and increased respiratory, and other infections.

6. Standardized assessment with the PEDI (Haley et al. 1989), VABS (Sparrow et al. 1984), and PDMS (Folio and Fewell 1983) would be appropriate.

8. Teaching and learning activities of daily living within a behavioral frame of reference. Developmental frame of reference to address sensorimotor, cognitive, and psychosocial aspects. Human occupation frame of reference also could be used.

10. Helene is participating in a continuous quality improvement (CQI) process to improve service efficiency, effectiveness, and value. This process includes a series of mechanisms used to identify opportunities for positive change. Total quality management (TQM) is an operational style that enables the CQI process.

Heidi

2. Many children with spina bifida require shunts as hydrocephalus occurs in 70% to 86% of cases. Signs of shunt malfunction are the same as clinical signs of increased intracranial pressure. Infants and toddlers with increased intracranial pressure may be lethargic, irritable and may have problems with reflexes, feeding, and muscle tone. Sunsetting eyes and vomiting are common. Older children may experience vomiting, headaches, lethargy, or irritability. Refer to Tappit-Emas 1994 Table 5-1, p.149.

4. Erickson's Industry versus Inferiority stage is characterized by mastery of peer group activities and the transfer of security from the family to the social peer group. Havighurst suggests the middle childhood is a time when individuals develop physical skills for games; wholesome attitudes towards themselves, social groups and institutions; interpersonal skills; skills in reading, writing, and calculation; and activities of daily living concepts. These developmental challenges are Heidi's.

6. The physical, social, and cultural contexts of occupational performance can positively and negatively impact Heidi. Community access and physical layout of the swimming pool, school, and playground should be investigated. Social acceptance from Anna positively influences Heidi, but the social expectations placed on Heidi by her teacher may not be appropriate, as they are not congruent with her potential. The value that Mother places on informed decision making will benefit Heidi, as her family continues to advocate on her behalf.

8. Heidi's strengths and abilities allow for compensation and new learning. Her motivational style will be important throughout life.

10. Heidi's visual perceptual score (perceptual quotient or standard score = 76) and visual motor score (standard score = 55) are approximately 2 and 3 standard deviations, respectively, below the mean. The TVPS (Gardner 1982) visual perceptual score would be a less significant finding if Heidi's IQ score were 1 standard deviation below the mean, as it would be congruent with her overall functioning.

12. Assuming parent agreement, goals must include *at a minimum*: providing a wheelchair cushion, improving handwriting, learning self catheterization and advanced wheelchair transfers for swimming, and further assessing fine-motor coordination, strength and the impact of visual perceptual functioning on classroom and academic performance. A referral to speech therapy for screening of language is appropriate.

14. A commercial cushion with foam for incontinence is appropriate. Alternatively, a lightweight gel cushion is appropriate.

16. Write your own screening report. Try using the format shown in the *Antonio* or *Robert* cases or the suggestions incorporated into *Pierre*.

Tim (Part 1)

2. There is clinical evidence of motor and postural dysfunction with incoordination and inattention. For example, Mr. L. reports "too active," "clumsy," inefficient ways of doing things. Tim demonstrates perpetual disorganization, fine motor incoordination and possible dyspraxia. He has difficulty manipulating objects, drops items, falls off desk chair, trips over balls, etc. He avoids climbing, jumping, etc. See Appendix D for COMPS (Wilson et al. 1994) results.

4. School-based service would reference Public Law 101–476 for a definition of *learning disability*. There is some evidence to support this diagnosis. More conclusive psychological and language testing would be required for diagnoses.

6. Eligibility under Public Law 101–476 would be jointly established by the occupational therapist and educational specialists. Coverage of students with attention deficit disorders was introduced into public law in this 1990 Amendment. Tim's physician also may consider a developmental coordination disorder diagnosis.

8. The caseload formulas in AOTA (1989) would indicate that Meredith will use 22.5 hours per week, on average, providing services to her current caseload.

$$1.25 (15) + 0.625 (4) + 0.625 (2) = 22.5$$

10. Although Mr. L.'s statement may portray his preference for segregation, Public Law favors inclusion in normal and integrated educational settings.

12. Direct service and consultation to Mr. L., if approved, and time available on caseload; otherwise, a need is established for consultation at a minimum. Evaluation would be more complete with perceptual, visual motor, and sensory integration testing with the TVPS (Gardner 1988), TVMS-R (Gardner 1995), SIPT (Ayres 1989), and (or) the *Bruininks-Oseretsky Test of Motor Proficiency* (Bruininks 1978).

Tim (Part II)

2. Six SIPT (Ayres 1989) patterns are described in Kramer and Hinojosa (1993, p.89). Clients with this diagnosis have the greatest difficulty with praxis on verbal command and static and dynamic balance. See Kramer and Hinojosa (1993, p. 90) or Case-Smith et al. (1996, p. 346).

4. Remedial recommendations could include improving praxis, balance, and sensory processing and integration, while functional recommendations might include environmental modifications and teaching Mr. L. different methods of interacting.

6. Provide Mr. L. with behavior management strategies. See Jones (1991, pp. 57–63); Warger and Heflin (1994, Chapters 4 and 5).

Robert

2. Robert appears to be a very industrious 8 year old who enjoys sports and outdoor play, as evidenced by his entrepreneurial savings, leisure interests, academic accomplishments and contributions to home management. His time commitments between student, friend, and son roles will change throughout the year. School will resume upon discharge. Dysfunction is evident in all occupational performance components, impacting success in all premorbid activities, tasks, and roles.

4. Both illustrations indicate left neglect. Homonomous hemianopsia screening is required. The drawing of a person is immature. Initially, he forgot 7 on the clock, suggesting inattention or sequencing memory problems.

6. Mother may continue to require your support, particularly regarding education concerning TBI sequelae. The *Canadian Occupational Performance Measure* (COPM) (Law et al. 1994) would be useful to identify and prioritize Robert's and Mother's concerns.

8. Review Kramer and Hinojosa (1993, pp. 332–344).

10. Review Kramer and Hinojosa (1993, pp. 69–83); and Boehm (1988).

12. Plan your own meaningful and purposeful activity for Robert.

14. Completion of full *Bruininks-Oseresky Test of Motor Proficiency* (Bruininks 1978) is appropriate. The subtest Running Speed and Agility may not be appropriate until safe to administer.

Gail (Natalie and Ali)

2. Reflex inhibiting pattern (RIP) includes forearm supination; wrist and finger extension; and finger and thumb abduction. Although portions of the RIP are incorporated into a number of the designs, the spasticity reduction splint incorporates the entire pattern.

4. Tardier et al. 1979 suggests that muscle fibre length, sarcomere length and number, and muscle spindle calibration can be "reset" by prolonged lengthening.

6. Information shared with parents includes purpose and care of the splint, application and positioning, splint cleaning, and wearing schedules. Skin inspection instructions and precautions. Ali will require special attention due to his communication abilities.

8. Try the short thumb opponens splint shown in Figure 5.23. By restricting Natalie's wrist, you have impaired functional performance. The tone reducing and joint positioning features of the thumb opponens or short opponens splint will still meet Natalie's needs.

10. Variables include choice of splint, wearing schedule, and compliance.

Dear Customer:

Thank you for purchasing this product. I'm sure it will become a valuable professional tool.

I'm interested in learning your opinion of this product. After you have used it for a few weeks, please complete the short questionnaire that follows. Then photocopy and send the questionnaire back to me either by fax (210-949-4452) or by mail: Communication/Therapy Skill Builders, 555 Academic Court, San Antonio, TX 78204-9941, Attn: Acquisitions.

Your comments help us to provide practical products suited to your professional needs.

Sincerely,

Aurelio Prifitera

Aurelio Prifitera, President
Communication/Therapy Skill Builders,
A Harcourt Health Sciences Company
555 Academic Court
San Antonio, Texas 78204-2498

---

1. Product Name:_____

2. Product ISBN: **07616** ___ ___ ___ ___ ___ (located on the copyright page)

3. Who uses the product (SLP, OT, PT, educator, other)? _____

4. In what type of setting (public school, private school, other) and with what clients do you work?

   _____

   _____

5. How often do you use this product? _____

Circle the most appropriate: HIGHEST◄──►LOWEST

   6. Is it up to date with current theory and guidelines?   5   4   3   2   1
   7. Does it provide helpful information?   5   4   3   2   1
   8. Is it easy to find the information you need?   5   4   3   2   1
   9. Does this product fill the need you anticipated it would?   5   4   3   2   1

Please comment briefly:

   10. What do you like most about this product? _____

   _____

   _____

   11. How would you improve it? _____

   _____

   _____

   *signature (optional)*_____

QUESTIONNAIRE